TRACING
LEEDS
ANCESTORS

FAMILY HISTORY FROM PEN & SWORD

Tracing Your Army Ancestors
Simon Fowler

Tracing Your Pauper Ancestors
Robert Burlison

Tracing Your Yorkshire Ancestors
Rachel Bellerby

Tracing Your Air Force Ancestors
Phil Tomaselli

Tracing Your Northern Ancestors
Keith Gregson

Tracing Your Black Country Ancestors
Michael Pearson

Tracing Your Textile Ancestors
Vivien Teasdale

Tracing Your Railway Ancestors
Di Drummond

Tracing Secret Service Ancestors
Phil Tomaselli

Tracing Your Police Ancestors
Stephen Wade

Tracing Your Royal Marine Ancestors
Richard Brooks
and Matthew Little

Tracing Your Jewish Ancestors
Rosemary Wenzerul

Tracing Your East Anglian Ancestors
Gill Blanchard

Tracing Your Ancestors
Simon Fowler

Tracing Your Liverpool Ancestors
Mike Royden

Tracing Your Scottish Ancestors
Ian Maxwell

Tracing British Battalions on the Somme
Ray Westlake

Tracing Your Criminal Ancestors
Stephen Wade

Tracing Your Labour Movement Ancestors
Mark Crail

Tracing Your London Ancestors
Jonathan Oates

Tracing Your Shipbuilding Ancestors
Anthony Burton

Tracing Your Northern Irish Ancestors
Ian Maxwell

Tracing Your Service Women Ancestors
Mary Ingham

Tracing Your East End Ancestors
Jane Cox

Tracing the Rifle Volunteers
Ray Westlake

Tracing Your Legal Ancestors
Stephen Wade

Tracing Your Canal Ancestors
Sue Wilkes

Tracing Your Rural Ancestors
Jonathan Brown

Tracing Your House History
Gill Blanchard

Tracing Your Tank Ancestors
Janice Tait and David Fletcher

Tracing Your Family History on the Internet
Chris Paton

Tracing Your Medical Ancestors
Michelle Higgs

Tracing Your Second World War Ancestors
Phil Tomaselli

Tracing Your Channel Islands Ancestors
Marie-Louise Backhurst

Tracing Great War Ancestors DVD
Pen & Sword Digital &
Battlefield History TV Ltd

Tracing Your Prisoner of War Ancestors: The First World War
Sarah Paterson

Tracing Your British Indian Ancestors
Emma Jolly

Tracing Your Naval Ancestors
Simon Fowler

Tracing Your Huguenot Ancestors
Kathy Chater

Tracing Your Servant Ancestors
Michelle Higgs

Tracing Your Ancestors from 1066 to 1837
Jonathan Oates

Tracing Your Merchant Navy Ancestors
Simon Wills

Tracing Your Lancashire Ancestors
Sue Wilkes

Tracing Your Ancestors through Death Records
Celia Heritage

Tracing Your West Country Ancestors
Kirsty Gray

Tracing Your First World War Ancestors
Simon Fowler

Tracing Your Army Ancestors – 2nd Edition
Simon Fowler

Tracing Your Irish Family History on the Internet
Chris Paton

Tracing Your Aristocratic Ancestors
Anthony Adolph

Tracing Your Ancestors from 1066 to 1837
Jonathan Oates

TRACING YOUR LEEDS ANCESTORS

A Guide for Family Historians

Rachel Bellerby

Pen & Sword
FAMILY HISTORY

First published in Great Britain in 2015
PEN & SWORD FAMILY HISTORY
an imprint of
Pen & Sword Books Ltd
47 Church Street,
Barnsley
South Yorkshire,
S70 2AS

Copyright © Rachel Bellerby, 2015

ISBN 978 1 47382 800 1

The right of Rachel Bellerby to be identified as Author of the Work has been asserted by her in accordance with the Copyright, Designs and Patents Act 1988.

A CIP catalogue record for this book is available from the British Library.

All rights reserved. No part of this book may be reproduced or transmitted in any form or by any means, electronic or mechanical including photocopying, recording or by any information storage and retrieval system, without permission from the Publisher in writing.

Typeset in Palatino and Optima by CHIC GRAPHICS

Printed and bound in England by
CPI Group (UK), Croydon, CR0 4YY

Pen & Sword Books Ltd incorporates the imprints of Pen & Sword Archaeology, Atlas, Aviation, Battleground, Discovery, Family History, History, Maritime, Military, Naval, Politics, Railways, Select, Social History, Transport, True Crime, Claymore Press, Frontline Books, Leo Cooper, Praetorian Press, Remember When, Seaforth Publishing and Wharncliffe.

For a complete list of Pen & Sword titles please contact
PEN & SWORD BOOKS LTD
47 Church Street, Barnsley, South Yorkshire, S70 2AS, England
E-mail: enquiries@pen-and-sword.co.uk
Website: www.pen-and-sword.co.uk

CONTENTS

Introduction   vi

Chapter 1	A History of Leeds	1
Chapter 2	Leeds Family History Resources	14
Chapter 3	City of 1,000 Trades	26
Chapter 4	Street Life	39
Chapter 5	Education	56
Chapter 6	Migration and Poverty	66
Chapter 7	Religion	79
Chapter 8	Leisure Time	95
Chapter 9	Leeds Online	109
Chapter 10	Explore Bygone Leeds	122
Chapter 11	Leeds Directory	137

Conclusion   152
Reading List   153
Index   154

INTRODUCTION

The city of Leeds in West Yorkshire is home to some 750,000 people and is one of the five biggest cities in the UK. For centuries, Leeds has attracted incomers from across the UK and further afield; people drawn here by the city's plethora of trades, its position midway between the east and west coasts; and the easy access to the countryside of the Dales.

Tracing Your Leeds Ancestors is an adventure which can go way beyond discovering the birth, marriage and death records of your ancestors. As we'll discover throughout this book, there are hundreds of resources to help you find out where your ancestors would have lived, what the surrounding streets were like and what their schooling would have been. You can find out about your ancestor's place of work, what leisure pursuits they might have followed and the shops and markets they would have visited.

The city is home to a number of fine archives, libraries and museums, all of which will be explored through the coming themed chapters, which cover topics including education, housing, leisure time, poverty and immigration. From an archive devoted to the history of shopping through to a modern museum facility which holds more than one million historic Leeds-related items, we learn what material is available to you and how to make the most of it to really bring your research to life. And to help you take your research that little bit further, Chapter 10 is devoted to bygone Leeds through walking trails, museum trips and themed tours.

Don't worry, though, if you're not able to visit Leeds in person; there are plenty of ideas for online research – online family history research has never been so exciting and, with photographs, oral recordings and archive film, you can enjoy the city's history unfolding from the comfort of your own home.

Introduction

So, whether you're new to family history and curious to find out about what life was like in bygone Leeds or you're an experienced researcher looking to take your findings a stage further, there's plenty to explore here. So let's start our journey into the history of Leeds, the city of 1,000 trades.

Joseph Priestley, a prominent Leeds clergyman and scientist.

Chapter 1

A HISTORY OF LEEDS

In this chapter we take a broad-ranging look at how the town (and later the city) of Leeds developed from the first settlements on the bank of the River Aire, through the emergence of a settled market town, the boom years of the Industrial Revolution and on to the development of post-war Leeds.

The Earliest Settlement
Leeds began as a settlement named 'Loidis' which was part of the kingdom of Elmet, a kingdom roughly corresponding to the area of the West Riding. Within twenty years of the Norman Conquest of 1066, Leeds was a manor with a population of around 200 under the overlordship of a man named Ilbert de Lacy. In these early years, the area was predominantly agricultural: a mill, church and farm labourers working for a master.

The settlement stood beside the River Aire, close to where today's Leeds Minster stands, and extending outwards to the west. This spot was close to an important crossing point of the River Aire which was to prove so valuable to trade and industry in the centuries to come.

Leeds in the Middle Ages
The town's first charter was granted in 1207, but unlike some of its neighbours like York and Pontefract, Leeds had no key territorial advantages. There was no castle and the town didn't stand on a key trade route, although it did have the River Aire as a means of transport for trading activities.

Nevertheless, Leeds's position at roughly halfway between London and Edinburgh and between the east and west coasts meant that its potential for trading could not be overlooked, as would be proved during the centuries to come. Under the terms of the town's

Leeds Bridge, close to one of the earliest crossing points of the Aire.

charter, an organised community began to take shape, with a bailiff who oversaw a court of justice, the first streets developing around Briggate, and an organised market attended by those in the surrounding settlements.

Just before the Black Death in 1348, which is estimated to have wiped out up to half the UK's population, the parish of Leeds had around 1,000 inhabitants – 300 of whom lived in the town centre. This was a small settlement when compared with the likes of Yorkshire towns which are now themselves much smaller than Leeds, including Selby and Ripon.

The heart of life in Leeds during the medieval era was the land between Briggate, Kirkgate and the River Aire. After having passed through ownership of the de Gant family (who received the manor of Leeds after the Norman Conquest), Ranulf, Earl of Chester, and then the de Lacys, King Henry IV was the overlord of Leeds on his accession in 1399.

In the early Middle Ages, most wool was produced in the south of England. However by 1300, as guild regulations became stricter even in towns such as York and Beverley, northern wool producers began to move south to Leeds and the surrounding areas. By the early sixteenth century, whole families were involved in the production of wool – cleaning it, teazling it, spinning and then weaving. It was finally sent on to a fulling mill to be finished and then sold on. Leeds was particularly well known for the production of broadcloth – a cheap but good quality textile.

By the Tudor period, Leeds was known as a textile town, helped no doubt by the presence of nearby Kirkstall Abbey, a large wool producer and trader. However, until the thirteenth century, wool was only produced on a small scale, for those who would be using it themselves.

In 1533, the town was described in *The Annals of Yorkshire* as being

> two miles lower than Christal Abbey, on Aire river, is a praty market, having one paroche churche reasonably well buildid, and as large as Bradford, but not so quik as it.

War and Plague

Leeds received its royal charter in 1626, just twenty years before some of the most horrific years in its history. The middle of the seventeenth century was a traumatic time in Leeds, with the town being affected by the Civil War, and then by the plague.

At the start of the Civil War, Leeds was under Royalist control but in January 1643 faced an attack by 1,500 men under the command of Sir Thomas Fairfax during which 500 prisoners were taken. The shattered town was laid low once again in 1645 when plague struck Leeds and killed 1,300 people between March and December.

Leeds as a Centre for Trade and Industry

Seventeenth-century Leeds centred on the thoroughfares of Briggate, Boar Lane and Kirkgate, with few buildings south of the river – a situation that would change dramatically with the coming of the Industrial Revolution and the growth of the textile and engineering industries.

Now a busy area of modern office blocks and chic boutique hotels, The Calls in the 1600s was described by historian Percy Robinson (writing in 1926) as 'an open space with orchards and a pleasant footpath along the riverside to the church'. The area which would later become the suburb of Burley was 'a remote village', and Park Lane was a country road bordered by fields.

By the eighteenth century Leeds was gaining a reputation for industry, with Daniel Defoe describing the town's 'inexhaustible stores' of coal. This fuel would prove crucial to the town's role in the coming Industrial Revolution.

In 1700, Leeds became an inland port, as the River Aire was made navigable from Leeds Bridge to the east, as part of the Aire & Calder Navigation. This meant that a coast-to-coast navigable waterway ran from Liverpool to Hull, with all the advantages to trade that this brought to the towns along the way, as they now could ship goods both in and out of the country.

In the busy streets of the core of town, as small as it was then compared to now, inns were plentiful and popular and were regarded as places for conducting business just as much as they were valued for leisure pursuits. The Kings Arms on Briggate and the White Swan at Kirkgate were two of the longest established – the Kings Arms was one of the city's oldest coaching inns, whilst the White Swan is still in existence, enjoying a busy position adjacent to the City Varieties Music Hall.

Briggate was a focal point for displays and parades, with townspeople enjoying bonfires on civic occasions and religious festivals. In the early eighteenth century, cockfighting took place at Chapeltown Moor, where there was also a popular horse fair upon which bets were placed. There were other cockfighting pits at the Talbot and the Rose & Crown inns in Briggate.

Ralph Thorseby's *Ducatus Leodunsis*, published in 1715, gave the most detailed account of the town since the Domesday Survey. Throesby described the abbey ruins with their mills for grinding corn. Mills were also mentioned at Armley and we are told that

Hunslet was 'chiefly inhabited by clothiers', with nearby Farnley having plenty of stone and coal. In 1726, cartographer John Cossins produced a map known as 'A new and exact plan of the town of Leeds' which captured a moment in time before the town changed forever with the beginnings of heavy industry and textile production in the century that followed.

The eighteenth century saw the town's potential to trade with distant markets expand with the establishment of the first horse and coach service between Leeds and London, 'flying machines on steel springs', which advertised services between London and Leeds in three days.

The first coach service to London operated on 19 May 1760 and the reality of the journey makes for sobering reading: a traveller would leave London at dawn, around 5am and spend the first night after a day on the road at Northampton. There would be further nights spent in Nottingham and Sheffield, before the weary journey finally came to an end on the late evening of the fourth day, when Leeds was finally reached.

An End to Domestic Industry
After centuries of industries flourishing in households alongside the River Aire, the domestic system of manufacturing began to come to an end as firms such as Marshalls (linen) and Gotts (wool) were established in the early nineteenth century. The demand for machinery to run the burgeoning textile trade stimulated an engineering industry in Leeds, with the associated development of trade in coal and iron as well as the growth of a fledgling railway industry.

Railways came to Leeds early, with the opening in 1811 of a railway at Middleton Colliery, which had been a coal mine since the thirteenth century. The railway ran from Middleton to Leeds Bridge and could pull up to thirty wagons at thirty miles an hour. A public railway service in the town followed in 1834; beginning at precisely 6.30am on 22 September, when the first line from Marsh Lane station in Leeds to Selby opened, running one train per day initially, which served both passengers and goods traffic.

Within fifteen years, Leeds had four different railways – Midland

Sir Titus Salt, founder of Saltaire Mills, born in Morley in 1803. © Library of Congress, digital id: cph.3c28482.

Railway opened in 1842, Leeds & Bradford in 1846, the Great Northern in 1848 and the Leeds, Dewsbury & Manchester the same year.

A History of Leeds

Victorian Leeds

One of the most vibrant and memorable eras in the history of Leeds was the Victorian age, when key buildings such as the Town Hall and Civic Hall were built, industry was booming and Leeds achieved city status. But behind the splendour, life for thousands of Leeds inhabitants was merely a struggle for survival, with substandard housing, little or no education and poor working conditions.

At the start of the Victorian period, the population of Leeds was 150,000 and by the end of the nineteenth century this figure was approaching half a million. Textiles, engineering and printing all attracted incomers in their thousands, from across the UK and overseas.

Leeds in 1866.

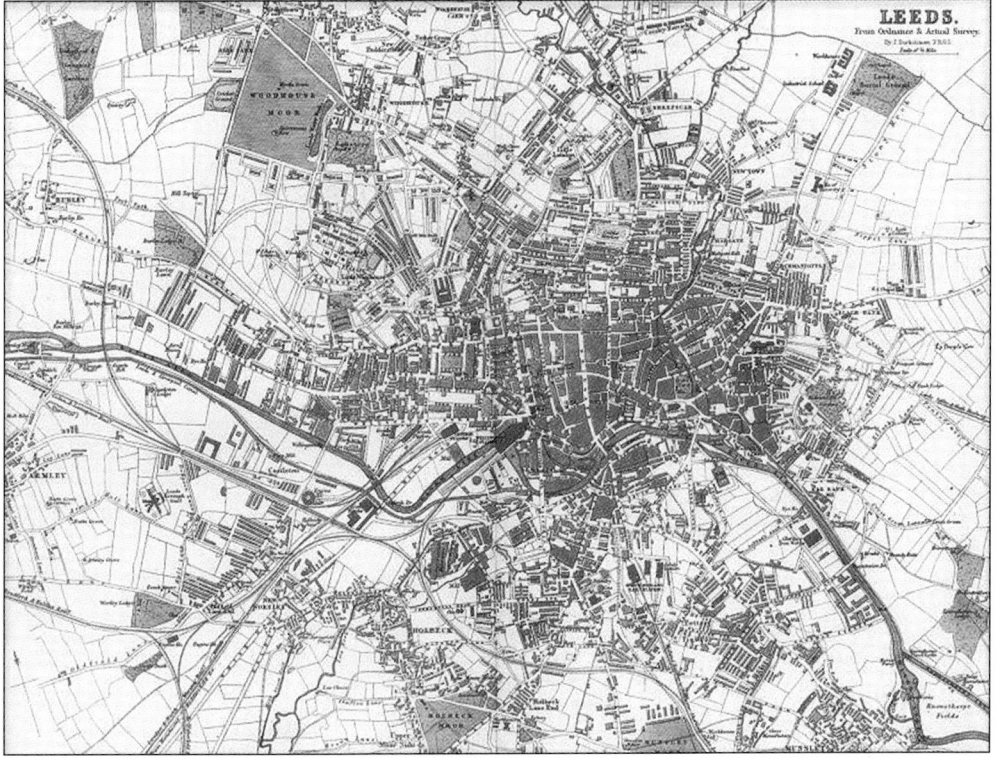

Leeds Town Hall, built in 1858. © Tuck DB Postcards.

The town's growing wealth and population was given a focus when Leeds Town Hall was built in 1858, replacing the Moot Hall on Briggate as a centre of administration and a symbol of local pride.

The Town Hall, which was designed by Cuthbert Brodick, cost £132,000 to build and was opened by Queen Victoria, with local mills coming to a close for the day in celebration. Such was the interest in the opening that an official report recorded that 'at the town hall the crowds were so great that the barriers seemed quite inadequate and last cracked and splintered before the immense pressure'. Since its official opening the Town Hall has served its citizens through a variety of uses including council business, a police station, concert hall and court. Some 150 years on, it is for many a true symbol of Leeds life.

Within three years of the creation of the Town Hall, the Corn

Exchange, Leeds Civic Theatre and Leeds Mechanics' Institute had been added to the list of landmarks. A big turning point for Leeds was when the town gained city status in 1893. In a show of civic pride, the City Council decreed that this brand-new city should have buildings befitting its new status and among the new creations were a large domed roof for Kirkgate Market and a new market hall.

Leeds in the First World War

In comparison with other industrial cities such as Hull and Sheffield, Leeds suffered relatively lightly in terms of air raid casualties. However the city paid a high price in terms of servicemen and women killed, with the Leeds Pals battalion particularly badly hit. The Leeds Pals was formed in September 1914, weeks after the outbreak of the First World War and was officially named the 15th Battalion (1st Leeds), The Prince of Wales' Own West Yorkshire Regiment. Members of the battalion took part in the disastrous Battle of the Somme, with 528 casualties.

At the outbreak of war in August 1914, Leeds moved quickly from a peacetime industrial output into a wartime role. The Leeds Munitions Company was formed within a few weeks and the Leeds Forge Company began to manufacture shells, with two further sites added in Hunslet and Horsforth.

The National Shell Filling Factory was established in August 1915 at Barnbow near Crossgates, with the finished goods being transported from a hastily constructed Shell Factory station into the city by train. The workers were drafted in from Leeds and nearby towns including Wakefield, York, Tadcaster and Selby. At the height of production in the summer of 1916, some 16,000 workers were employed. Although it was kept secret at the time for reasons of morale and national security, the factory suffered a terrible tragedy when an explosion in November 1916 killed thirty-five female workers.

Leeds in the Second World War

At the outbreak of the Second World War in 1939, the city of Leeds was in a strong position in terms of manufacture, and the textile and engineering industries were to prove vital to the war effort.

The Vickers Armstrong factory which was established in Leeds produced thousands of guns and tanks, aided in armament making by other firms including Avro (at the current Leeds/Bradford airport) and Blackburns.

A highly skilled textiles and engineering workforce switched to war work, for example, with engineering firms switching to making shells, fuses and field guns. Tanks were made at the Royal Ordnance Factory Barnbow and at John Fowler's Steam Plough Works. Hunslet Engine Company remodelled a pre-war design to create an austerity shunter locomotive.

Burtons Tailors switched to uniform production and in a patriotic move typical of many large firms at the time, Charles H Roe Ltd, a carriage works, extended its production to convert the chassis of vehicles into ambulances, lorries and other vehicles to help in the war effort. In an effort to avoid the expected air raids, factory buildings were camouflaged and windows blocked for the blackout, although Leeds escaped the major bombing that hit cities such as London and Liverpool.

Emergency measures relating to public safety began within weeks of war breaking out. On 31 August 1939 sandbags were placed at important public buildings including the Civic Hall, Town Hall and even the ground floor of the Quarry Hill flats. In anticipation of high numbers of casualties should the city be bombed, the water was taken out of municipal pools at Armley and Bramley and their floors covered over, in order to convert them into first aid facilities.

One of the biggest tragedies to hit Second World War Leeds was the Leeds Blitz, nine air raids which took place from 14 to 15 March 1941. Around forty enemy bombers dropped incendiary bombs on the city and hit targets including the Town Hall, the train station, Kirkgate Market, Leeds Museum and the Quarry Hill flats. More than sixty people were killed and over 100 homes destroyed.

Help was at hand when it was needed. Thirteen Women's Voluntary Service depots had been established in the city to feed and clothe those affected by air raids – these sites included Harehills Congregational Sunday School and the Salem Chapel on Hunslet Lane.

World War Resources

There are many different avenues for exploring what life was during the two World Wars, both for those who lived through the war years in the city and for those Leeds men and women who served their country. Local newspapers offer a picture of wartime life, through news reports on local matters such as arrangements for air raid precautions, evacuation and the shelter of refugees.

These newspapers also carried wartime news, following the progress of the war overseas, for the benefit of those at home, as well as photographs and obituaries of those killed in action. Such records are particularly poignant after major battles such as the Somme, when pages and pages of obituaries are a sober reminder of what the war cost the city and countless other communities across the country.

You can access wartime newspapers online, at Leeds Local & Family History Library. WYAS Leeds has newspaper cuttings, wartime memories and records of national and local wartime administration, including leaflets and posters issued to householders and businesses. For a First World War collection guide from WYAS, visit: http://bit.ly/myleedsww1.

WYAS Leeds holds a 1915–16 diary of Private Edward Woofenden of the 15th Yorkshire Regiment, Leeds Pals. Also available for study are newspaper cuttings, memorial service details and correspondence relating to the Leeds Pals Association from 1924 to 1954.

The Leodis website (www.leodis.net) has many images of wartime damage and rescue works, as well photos of celebrations for the end of war.

The Leeds War Memorial

Leeds Local & Family History Library holds a book of memorial press cuttings (LQ94046LEE) which are full of details of the city's attempts to create a memorial to the fallen of the First World War, in the years following the conflict. The volume contains many dozens of letters from correspondents to newspapers, offering their ideas as to what a suitable tribute should be and where it should be sited.

The Leeds War Memorial remembers the dead of the two World Wars.

Eventually, the monument was dedicated on 14 October 1922 in a ceremony presided over by Lord Lascelles. A local paper reported:

> Truly the heart of the big industrial city was around the war memorial this afternoon. The people came from every corner of Leeds and as the hour for the unveiling of the memorial drew nigh, multitudes were beginning to assemble in the vicinity.

The memorial originally stood in City Square, near the railway station, and is now on the Headrow, beside the city's art gallery.

Post-War Leeds

In common with other major northern cities such as Bradford and Manchester, the textile trade in Leeds began a slow decline in the years following the First World War. Competition from overseas meant that buyers could purchase cheaper imports, although Leeds, 'the city that makes everything', retained its prosperity to some extent through its hundreds of trades, including footwear, engineering and chemicals.

As the twentieth century progressed, the city's entrepreneurial spirit continued and new trades including retail, media and, most recently, e-commerce and banking, emerged. The final years of the twentieth century saw great changes to a cityscape which had, in essence, changed little since the Victorian age. Apartment blocks and soaring office complexes were built on the site of former mills, factories and slum areas.

Leeds is now recognised, as it has been for well over a century, as one of the most prosperous and forward-thinking cities in the north of England. What will our descendants write about the coming years when the history of twenty-first-century Leeds is recorded?

Chapter 2

LEEDS FAMILY HISTORY RESOURCES

This chapter explores the various options available to you when researching your Leeds ancestors. The first section outlines the main archive and library resources, whilst the second takes a wide-ranging view of the different types of material that you can work with. Then, as we move through the following chapters, more specialised archives and resources are introduced.

Libraries and Archives

Leeds Local & Family History Library
Leeds Local & Family History Library (Leeds L&FHL) is on the second floor of Leeds Central Library, next to the Town Hall. This is the perfect starting point for beginners to family history and/or the history of Leeds. This specialist library is home to several large rooms of books, maps, magazines and periodicals.

A good place to start on a first visit to the library is the information desk where you can find leaflets and research guides to take away or use during your time at the library. The library is keen to welcome researchers of all levels of experience and runs monthly beginners workshops as well as regular workshops on how to use the Ancestry website, to which Leeds Library card holders have free access.

Staff are happy to answer basic research queries and, for more lengthy questions, offer a paid research service and paid one-to-one sessions with library staff. You don't have to live in Leeds to access the research service; the staff regularly handle queries from around the country and overseas.

The Local & Family History Library is housed within Leeds Central Library, next to the Town Hall.

The library has thousands of items relating to life in the city over the centuries and the online index (www.leedslocalindex.net) is just the starting point, as a large proportion of the material held doesn't appear on here as yet. Staff are regularly indexing the holdings as new material is acquired or assessed.

A particularly topical collection in the years of the First World War Centenary (from 2014 to 2018) is the library's war-related material. The absent voters lists show which servicemen were absent from their home address whilst on military service and include the serviceman's army number, his home address and details of any

Spotter and predictor operators at an anti-aircraft site in Leeds in 1941. © Imperial War Museum.

other people living at this address at the time. This information can be used in conjunction with electoral registers for the years before and after to follow a family in the years beyond the 1911 census, which is the most recent census available for study.

The Library is also strong on education records, with magazines and yearbooks for schools and further education establishments across the city including Leeds Grammar School (starting in the 1820s) and Leeds University. Education records are covered in more detail in Chapter 5.

The politics collection includes details of councillors and MPs during the nineteenth and twentieth centuries and political ephemera from the nineteenth century through to the present day. Even if your ancestor wasn't a councillor it can be very interesting to find out what issues mattered to voters at a particular point in time.

Businesses are also well represented, with company magazines for different Leeds firms (which staff are currently indexing), photographs and employee details. Many of those referred to within these publications are 'ordinary' employees rather than management; something which is fairly unusual with old business records.

Herbert Henry Asquith, Liberal Prime Minister (1908–1916), born in Morley, Leeds in 1852. © Library of Congress, accession no. ggbain.23315.

Another rich source of information on specific people is the biographical material which the library holds. There are newspaper cuttings and obituaries relating to individuals from the nineteenth and twentieth centuries, as well as details of those Leeds servicemen who fought in the two World Wars and were mentioned in local newspapers. These can be searched via the online index (www.leedslocalindex.net).

One of the most popular library resources for family history researchers is the newspaper collection, which includes copies of the *Leeds Mercury* and the *Northern Star*. These can also be accessed online (www.leeds.gov.uk/onlineresources) if you have a Leeds Library card.

The map collection covers the whole of Yorkshire from the Ordnance Survey maps of 1850 through to the present day. Non-OS maps which focus on Leeds are also available and these are an interesting way of tracking the changing nature of a particular street or district, particularly if used in conjunction with trade directories to see patterns of trade and business.

West Yorkshire Archive Service Leeds

The Leeds Archives (WYAS Leeds) is part of West Yorkshire Archive Service, which has sister offices at Wakefield, Bradford, Kirklees and Calderdale. The Leeds branch is located at Morley, a small town between Leeds and Bradford, approximately five miles southwest of Leeds centre.

At the time of going to print, the office is open on Wednesday, Thursday and Friday, 9.30am to 5pm. Booking is desirable but not essential; however, as some material is kept offsite, it's advisable to make contact with staff if you'd like to see a specific collection. The catalogue for the Leeds archives is available online (http://catalogue.wyjs.org.uk) and you'll need a CARN readers' ticket if you're planning a visit to the archives, or you can apply for one in person on the day of your visit if you bring along ID.

The office has a number of catalogues and indexes, and staff are happy to talk through how best to find a particular item if you're unsure. Documents can be requested from the archive stores between 9.30am and 12 noon, and from 2pm and 4pm. You can request up to four documents at a time, and once you've finished with those, you can request more.

Staff at the Leeds office of WYAS (and its sister offices) are keen to welcome visitors at all stages in their family history research and as well as its hundreds of thousands of Leeds-related items, the archive also has a large library of Leeds history books.

WYAS as a whole is currently working on making its most popular collections available online, and every few months the website (http://www.archives.wyjs.org.uk) has information on the newest material, or you can sign up to a regular e-newsletter.

One of the most recent projects has been the release online (via Ancestry – which you can also access at any of the WYAS offices) of reformatory school records. Also available are prisoner records for 1801 to 1914 for HMP Wakefield, and West Riding and County borough police records for 1833 to 1914.

Yorkshire Archaeological Society

A short walk from Leeds Town Hall is the headquarters of the

Leeds Family History Resources

Yorkshire Archaeological Society (YAS), a society founded in 1863 to promote the study of the county's past. The society's library of books has been built up over more than a century and is open to researchers by appointment.

Among the most useful resources for anyone with Leeds ancestors are books relating to the history of the city, industry, copies of the *Yorkshire Archaeological Journal*, and Wakefield Court Rolls. YAS members can borrow books free of charge (after paying an annual £1 borrowing fee). The library catalogue takes the form of a card index which is available to consult on the premises.

The archives, kept in the same building, comprise material donated to the society over the years. As well as family archives and estate papers, there are also wills, manorial court rolls and transcripts of parish registers. Some of the holdings of the YAS archives are listed online at Access to Archives (http://www.nationalarchives.gov.uk/a2a) and on the WYAS website (http://catalogue.wyjs.org.uk) and there are plans to list all holdings within the near future. Parish register transcripts, monumental inscriptions and building reports are listed on the society's website (https://www.yas.org.uk/content/archives.html).

Most of the library material, including books and pamphlets, can be accessed via a card catalogue. Although staff are in the process of creating an online catalogue, for now the card version remains the main route into exploring the collections. You'll need to inventive in your searches – for example, if searching for records relating to the suburb of Hunslet, not only should you search the cards under 'H' but also under the subject area of your search, such as 'burials', 'births', 'industry', etc.

There are several study areas for those undertaking their own research and staff run weekly tours of the society's archive holdings as well as help sessions, aimed both at beginners and those who've hit a brick wall in their research.

The society has large collections of family history publications from family history societies across Yorkshire and further afield, as well as collections of material published by the Thoresby Society, which also has rooms in the building.

There is a long run of the *Leeds Mercury* and a large collection of pamphlets of interest to local historians, including histories produced for or by local churches, societies and clubs.

In the archives section, the YAS also has its own publishing arm of record series, and the collections relating to the histories of local families (produced both privately and commercially) are extremely useful. Unpublished material held by YAS includes monumental inscriptions which are still in the process of being compiled, and transcripts of parish registers. There are also maps, plans, deeds and wills, as well as manorial court rolls for the Leeds area.

The YAS website (http://bit.ly/myleedsyasarchive) includes an overview of the collection, a guide to the holdings and advice on what the different records offer.

Basic Resources for Tracing Leeds Ancestors

Census returns
Census returns, one of the most useful resources for tracing Leeds (and other UK) ancestors, are a ten-yearly record of the place where each person in the UK was present on the day the census was taken. These returns are such a useful record because not only do they give the address where an ancestor resided on a given night at ten-year intervals, they also (unlike many records such as voters' lists) give details of each member of the household rather than just the head of the house.

The first returns available are for the year 1841 and this set is the least detailed, giving only names, ages (rounded down to the nearest five years for those aged 15 or under), occupations and whether the person was born in Yorkshire.

From 1851 through to 1911 (the last census currently available for research), you can see the name of each householder, their relationship (if any) to the head of house, occupation and town of birth. And if your ancestor was in a children's home, prison, workhouse or other institution at the time of the census, they will be listed under that address.

Leeds L&FHL has microfilm copies of census returns for Leeds and the rest of Yorkshire for 1841 through to 1911. You can also access all of these records as well as the 1911 census via Ancestry.com, which you can use free of charge at the library.

WYAS Leeds holds the originals of the only surviving pre-1841 census returns for Leeds – an incomplete Leeds township census for 1801, Farsley for 1811, and Yeadon for 1811, 1821 and 1831. For permission to search these returns, contact the WYAS Leeds office. The L&FH Library also has a microfilm copy of the 1801 township census and a transcript copy of the Calverley, Farsley and Yeadon census listed above.

If you're unsure where an ancestor lived, you can use the street and name indexes to the census returns up to 1901 at the Leeds L&FH Library.

Local newspapers

Local newspapers can be accessed in Leeds L&FHL, free of charge for anyone who visits in person, and also free to Leeds Library Card holders from their own home (at http://bit.ly/myleeds19thcentury). Here, you can browse through a whole century of indexed newspapers, printed both in Leeds and other large towns including Hull, Manchester and London.

Browse a century of old newspapers from your own home.

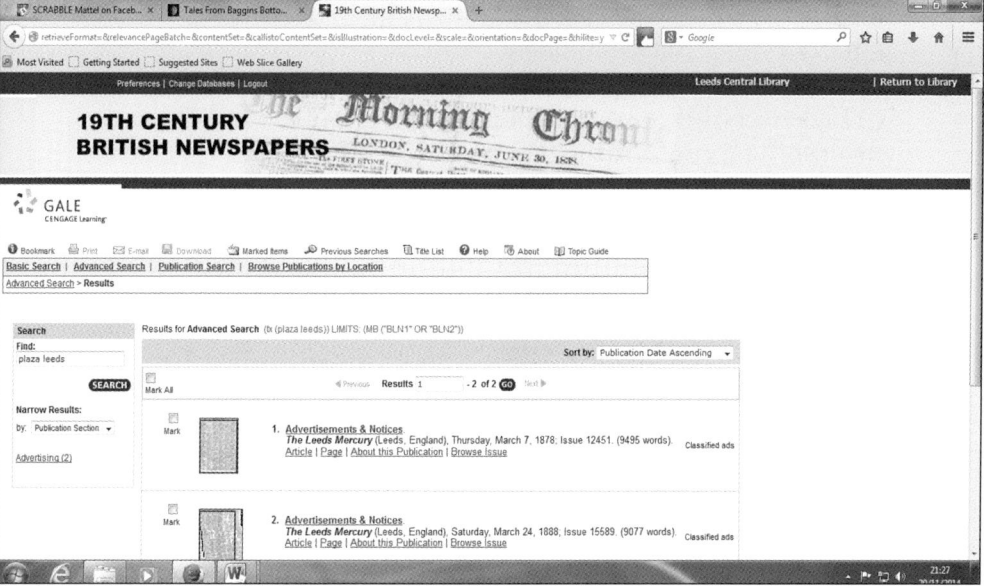

For other local newspaper resources, the Thoresby Society has transcribed and indexed decades-worth of the *Leeds Intelligencer* and *Leeds Mercury* which you can access by year in volumes – each of which is indexed by subject. Browsing through these for the years when your ancestors were in Leeds can give you a vivid idea of what life was like in the town, with the added bonus that you may find an ancestor or his or her street or place of work mentioned as you explore the records.

To give an idea of the type of information available, one day's worth of entries (13 November 1770) from the *Leeds Mercury* has news that 'On Wednesday last the Grand Canal from Leeds to Liverpool was begun at Halsall in Lancashire'. On the same day, the paper also reports the marriage of Robert Ramsbotham to Betty Swaine, 'a most amiable lady with a handsome fortune', and there are further details of the deaths of three Leeds dwellers, including Reverend Crooke, the vicar of Kippax and curate of Hunslet. And finally, notice is given of the availability of two 'handsome new built sashed houses in Boar Lane with large cellars'.

Trade directories
Trade directories are a useful resource for filling in gaps between censuses, as you may be able track where your ancestors were living from year to year, and also use the directories for local history purposes, in order to discover more about the character of a particular street and the different businesses which were there over the years.

Trade directories were created annually from around the mid-nineteenth century and their purpose was to allow townspeople to find tradesmen and women by trade or district, in a similar way to the way in which we'd use telephone directories nowadays. Leeds L&FHL has extensive collections of trade directories, which are on open access and which you can browse at leisure. They are shelved according to year, with many years covered by more than one directory.

The Kelly's Directory, which is generally the most comprehensive in its coverage, has alphabetical listings of townspeople, with surname and first name, next is the person's trade and finally their house number and street, making this section work as a local address book. Next, is a 'Leeds Trades' section where people are listed alphabetically within trades, which are also in alphabetical order. Again, the listings run by surname, first name, house number and street. Finally, the 'official directory' section is a snapshot of city life at a given time and is helpful for building up a picture of public facilities. Members of Parliament for the borough are listed by name, as are magistrates. There are also lists of council officers, members of the Leeds incorporated Chamber of Commerce and names of the Board of Guardians of the Leeds Poor Law Union.

Public parks are listed (there are twenty named in the district for 1902–3) and there are also listings of theatres and music halls, as well as a list of clubs including the Central Socialists Club, Chess Club, Athletics Society, Curling Society, Tennis Club and working men's clubs. Places of worship listings include the address, name of the worship leader, the curate, patrons and times of services. School details have the name of the school, the number of pupils on the roll, average attendance and the names of teachers.

Voting records

Another way to trace ancestors between censuses is to make use of voting records. Both Burgess Rolls and Registers of Electors can be studied on open access at Leeds L&FH Library. Electoral registers were compiled on an annual basis and so allow you to follow your ancestor more accurately between censuses. The first surviving West Yorkshire Electoral Register dates to 1840, and from 1885 the number of people covered by these records increases, as male tenants were able to vote as well as property owners.

The Burgess Rolls cover those with rated property, listed in alphabetical order by surname, first name, nature of property rated, house number and street name. Most listings are for houses, but there are also 'house and land' and 'house and shop' listings. You'll need to know which ward your ancestor lived in, or otherwise be prepared to check the listings for each ward.

The registers of electors show those entitled to vote within the borough of Leeds. These are alphabetical and listed by township with the surname, first name, town of abode, nature of qualification (house or house and land), then the street name (but no number).

Parish registers
These records can help you find out more about ancestors in the years before civil registration began in 1837. The minister of each parish kept records of the births, marriages and deaths which occurred within his parish and many of these have survived, allowing you to taken your search back decades further than before civil registration.

WYAS has been working with Ancestry to digitise and make available all but a few of the parish registers in its care (certain parishes in Bradford and Wakefield are exempted and these are listed on the WYAS website). Over nine million birth, marriages and death records for West Yorkshire are now available, with births covered from 1512 to 1910, marriages and banns from 1512 to 1935, deaths and burials from 1512 to 1985 and confirmations from 1859 to 1915. All of these records are indexed and you can, if you wish, see the original records at the relevant WYAS office.

Maps
Maps are an often underused resource for family history researchers. Both WYAS Leeds and Leeds L&FHL have large collections of maps. Other historic maps can be explored at Special Collections at Leeds University Library, the Thoresby Society and the Yorkshire Archaeological Society.

The earliest useful map of Yorkshire is the 1577 Saxton's map, the first such map which can be realistically used by researchers. Even this has its limitations, as it misses out the Temple Newsam estate, which is known to have existed at the time the map was produced. Because many maps were simply copied from earlier versions, errors do occur.

Ordnance Survey maps were first produced at the start of the nineteenth century, at the height of fears of an attack from France. Work on the first Ordnance Survey map for Yorkshire began in 1815 and these early OS maps can be very useful to researchers as they contain a greater level of detail than most such maps do today. Some of these are on a 1:500 scale (around ten feet per mile) covering many of the county's towns and villages.

Tithe award maps were produced following the Tithe Commutation Act of 1836 whereby the church became entitled to cash rather than goods in payment for tithes. Maps were produced showing who owned what land and what each landowner was farming, to prove what tithes were owed to the church. The tithe maps for Leeds are available online as part of the Leeds Tithe Map Project (www.tracksintime.wyjs.org.uk) which we explore in more detail in Chapter 9.

Law and order records
Nineteenth-century criminal records which concern Leeds residents have recently been digitised as part of a project launched by Ancestry and West Yorkshire Archive Service. You can access Ancestry free of charge at any of the WYAS offices and browse thousands of criminal records, including emotive records involving under-age 'criminals', such as 12-year-old Richard Cardwell who was sent to East Moor Community Home School for stealing a pigeon. There are also details of over 400,000 adult criminals, including name, age, occupation, sentence – and often background information and physical characteristics.

Quarter Sessions
The West Riding Quarter Session records, held at WYAS Wakefield, are among the largest and most complete set of such records in the country, and cover the Leeds area. Until the 1970s, the Quarter Sessions were the major criminal court in England and the thousands of records generated by the cases heard can be explored. The Wakefield records date from 1662 through to 1971 and comprise a huge variety of criminal cases, from those with serious punishments such as transportation through to minor disputes between neighbours.

Chapter 3

CITY OF 1,000 TRADES

From fulling, spinning and weaving to retail, engineering and call centres, Leeds has provided employment for those who live in the city and surrounding areas for centuries. Indeed, the reputation of Leeds as a place of plentiful employment has drawn incomers from around the country and later, around the world. Like many British cities, Leeds has had its times of boom and bust but has certainly lived up to its reputation as 'city of 1,000 trades'.

In this chapter we take a broad overview of the different sectors of employment and then look at how to find out where your ancestors may have worked and how to discover more about their place of employment and/or what working life would have been like in a particular trade.

As with all family history research, the amount of information you can discover about a place of employment depends upon many different factors, including what the type of work was, who the employer was and what job your ancestor did. For example, an ancestor who was the city's mayor or a councillor is likely to have left more of a paper trail for you to follow than someone who was employed at a mill on a temporary basis or who worked for an engineering company which no longer exists.

This chapter contains details of the history of some of the city's biggest names in textiles, brewing, engineering and retail, with details of how to trace ancestors who worked for these companies. As with all family history records, none of these archives were created with future family history researchers in mind. Nevertheless, they can contain a surprising amount of information if you're lucky enough to find an ancestor listed. And if not, don't despair, as company magazines, leaflets and brochures can go a long way

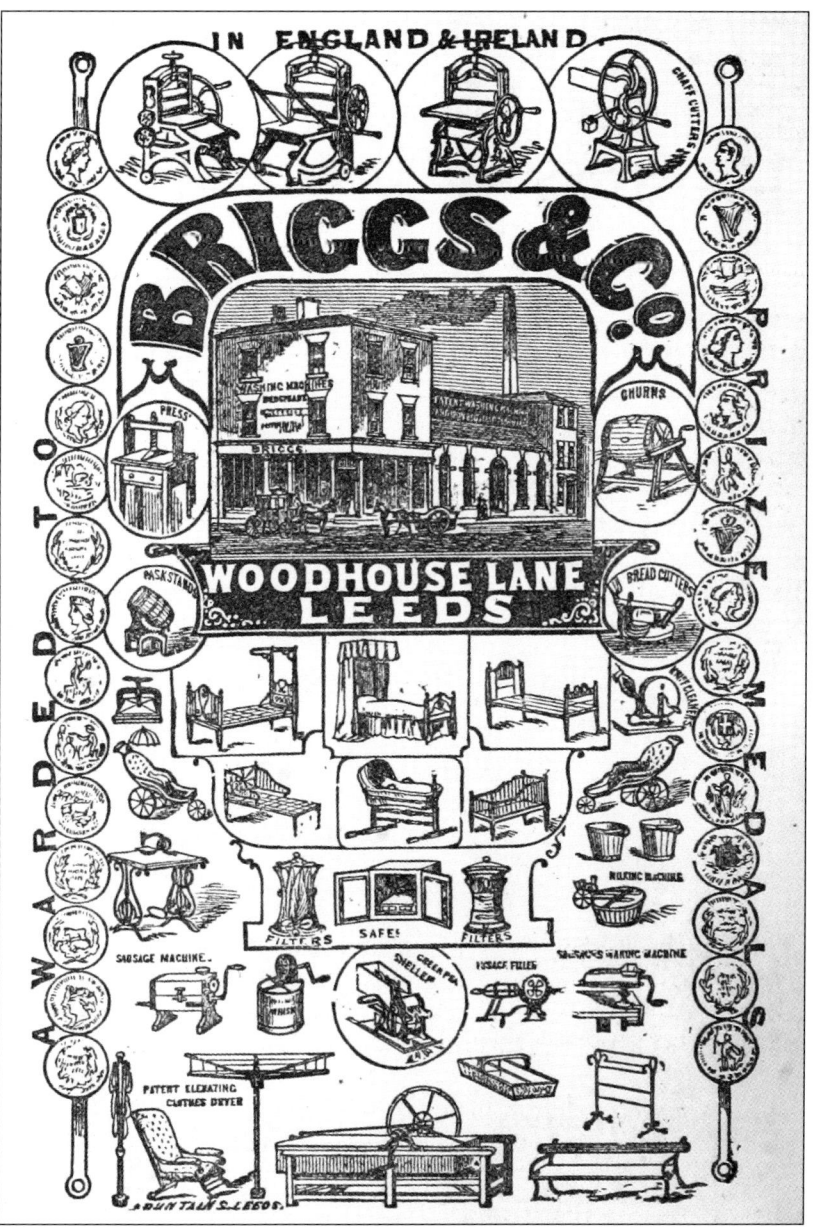

Thousands of companies have come and gone over the centuries,

towards showing you what a working environment was like and what kind of an employer your ancestor worked for.

The Textile Trade
Foremost among all of the Leeds trades is textiles, not only for its prominence in the region but because textiles is one of the city's oldest trades and has been the reason for the wealth and expansion of the area at different times in its history.

The soft water of the River Aire was ideal for cloth finishing and there is reference to a fulling mill at Temple Newsam as early as 1185. The medieval textile trade at this time was focused on small-scale output where workers produced cloth in their own homes, either selling the finished product on to a trader, or taking it to market themselves.

Leeds Bridge was the home of one of the city's largest medieval markets but by 1682 the cloth market had moved from its traditional position there to a more spacious site (for both traders and customers) on Briggate.

Author Daniel Defoe visited the first Leeds Cloth Market in 1724 and called it: 'A prodigy of its kind unequalled in the world'. By this time, the market was held twice a week, and Leeds and nearby Halifax could claim to be the largest cloth markets in the north of England. At this stage, one-sixth of all cloth exported from England was produced in Leeds and the suburb of Armley would soon become world famous for its textile mill.

Benjamin Gott's textile mill in Armley, which he established in 1804, helped the westward expansion of Leeds, with new mills soon following at Bramley, Pudsey and Farnley, allowing Leeds-based clothiers to move out of the town and into what were at the time villages (and are now suburbs) where they could carry out their textile work whilst enjoying the benefits of a semi-rural life with small-scale farming running alongside their textile production.

By this time, new textile technology such as John Kay's flying shuttle and James Hargreaves's spinning jenny had been in use in Leeds for over twenty years. Unlike the coming years of the Luddite movement, most home workers at this stage had no problem with

Benjamin Gott, the man who made Armley Mills into a world-class textile producer.

the new technology as it simply speeded up what they were doing at home rather than threatening their livelihood.

Within a few years, Gott had transformed his rundown mill into the largest wool factory in the world, which would pioneer new

Burton's Tailors was one of the city's biggest textile employers.

techniques of wool production, with power looms. The trend continued at nearby Temple Works and Marshall's Mill, both at Holbeck, which were two of the largest mills in the world; Temple Works had the largest individual room in the world in the Victorian age, where some 2,000 employees toiled to keep 7,000 spindles busy, whilst Marshall's was the largest flax mill in England.

Of course, once the textiles had been produced at these mills, someone needed to put them to good use. Although some was exported, much of what wasn't sold outside the area went on to be finished in Leeds, with the city's reputation as a centre for tailoring growing through the early twentieth century, with Burton's and Hepworth & Sons two of the biggest names.

Textile trade resources
The Yorkshire Industrial Heritage website (http://yorkshire.u08.eu/?t=leeds) has a map of Leeds textile mills of the past. If you're not sure which mill your ancestor might have worked in, the map will

help to pinpoint those closest to where the family lived, so that you can investigate the relevant records.

WYAS Leeds holds the records of dozens of textile firms which have deposited their records over the years. The archives of AW Hainsworth & Sons are a good example of the records available. They were a Leeds firm prominent in the textile trade and are a company which have weathered the downturn in the cloth trade in West Yorkshire and continue to operate today. The firm specialised in fine cloths which were used to cover snooker and pool tables and it may be this specialisation which enabled them to flourish where others failed or fell victim to foreign competition.

The company's records are held at WYAS Leeds under references WYL2139/WYL2325 and WYL1402 and so extensive are the archives that they were selected as one of the WYAS archive 'treasures'. The company was founded in 1783 by clothier Abimelech Hainsworth who initially worked on a small scale, using hand loom weavers and transporting the resulting cloth to the Leeds Coloured Cloth Hall himself. By the time of his death in 1836 he had amassed a fortune of £12,000 and owned a two-thirds share in Cape Mills in Farsley.

The business passed through the Hainsworth family and grew over the generations, with the company buying Temperance Mill in 1882 and Spring Valley Mill in 1889. Before they became known for producing snooker cloths, Hainsworths produced uniforms for the military, working through the two World Wars. A large fire destroyed their main mill in 1955 but the Hainsworths used the opportunity to make the move over to electric power.

The records at WYAS include archives relating to the company's Spring Valley Mills and Cape Mills, as well as over a century of correspondence, accounts, order books, personal Hainsworth family papers, letters and diaries. Archive material relating to employees includes wage books, warehouse books, sales day books and cloth sales ledgers. As with most employee records, it is rare for an individual employee to be named, but the books do give a wide overview of one of the city's largest and longest lived textile employers.

Another textile firm which is well represented at WYAS Leeds is

Burton's Tailors. Although originally based in Chesterfield, Burtons moved to Leeds in 1910 and has employed thousands of Leeds folk over the past century. The firm was famed as a good employer and the large Burton's factory on Hudson Road often welcomed sports stars and members of the royal family who were taken on tours of the facility, meeting workers along the way.

WYAS Leeds holds Burton's archives for 1896 to 1985 and these are classed as a 'treasure' of the service. The archive includes information on different branches of Burtons, trade union papers, photographs, adverts and training information.

Tetleys Breweries
The history of one of the city's best known companies, Tetley's Breweries, goes back to the 1740s and a man named William Tetley who was a Leeds brewster. The trade passed down to William's own son, also named William. However it was William junior's son Joshua who first expanded the firm.

In taking the risk of moving to new premises in the early 1820s, Joshua was breaking with family tradition and was on his own in the venture. On 9 November 1822 he placed an advert in the *Leeds Mercury* stating that he had taken over the brewery of a Mr Sykes in Salem Place on Hunslet Lane and 'spared no expense in selecting the best malt and hops'. Business

Tetley's is one of the best known Leeds firms.

was far from easy in the new location and his accounts show he paid £400 to Mr Sykes for the business and by the end of the first year of trading was showing a deficit of £2,700. In order to turn things around he was forced to move from his fine Georgian home on Park Square into industrial surroundings beside the brewery on Hunslet Lane. The sacrifice would pay off, though, as trade doubled the following year.

Within two generations, the company had become biggest brewery in the north, and by the mid-1870s, was producing over

170,000 barrels of beer per year. A striking art deco brewery was built for Tetley's in 1931 and this became the firm's headquarters.

By the 1960s, when the firm merged with Ind Coope of Burton on Trent and Ansells of Birmingham, there were more than 1,000 employees. The premises are no longer a working brewery and are now home to an art and learning centre.

Like the archives of Burton's Tailors, the Tetley Archives are classed as one of the 'treasures' of the West Yorkshire Archives Service. The archives include staff records, experiment books, mechanics' notebooks relating to the process of brewing and records of the staff members who served in the 7th Yorkshire, West Riding, (Leeds) Rifle Volunteer Corps. The full collections can be viewed online at WYAS under collection reference WYL756.

Railways and Engineering
As the home of the world's oldest continuously operating railway, Leeds has almost two centuries of railway and engineering heritage. The city's prominence in these two trades supported the textile industry in Leeds, with the latest developments in machinery used in mills across the city.

Middleton Railway, which is the world's oldest railway, passed across Hunslet Moor to the coal staithe close to Leeds Bridge. On 24 January 1812, the first commercially run steam locomotive gave its debut demonstration. The *Leeds Mercury* commented that 'fifty horses will be dispensed with, and we cannot forbear to hail the invention as a vast public utility'. The popular service ran through until the mid-twentieth century.

The first passenger railway in Leeds opened in 1834, when the Leeds & Selby railway was established with a terminus at Marsh Lane. This was followed by the North Midland Railway (1840) and the Manchester & Leeds Railway in 1854, which operated from Leeds Central Station.

Armley Industrial Museum
Despite its strong reputation for textiles (and its status as having once been the oldest woollen mill in the world) the Armley Industrial Museum is also home to collections of standard and narrow gauge

Leeds Central Station pictured in the 1960s © Ben Brooksbank caption.

rolling stock, along with a short line of track. These include the *Lord Granby*, built in 1902 by Hudswell Clarke and *Jack* from the Hunslet Engine Company which dates to 1898.
Website: bit.ly/myleedsarmley

Middleton Railway
Visit the world's oldest railway and see the remains of ancient coal workings in Middleton Woods. The railway operates steam engine rides and there is a museum at the station which is home to a collection of engines and rolling stock. Displays demonstrate how steam locomotive parts were built (most just a few miles from Middleton). Website: www.middletonrailway.org.uk

WYAS Leeds
The Leeds office of WYAS holds records relating to dozens of the city's engineering and railway companies, including Hunslet Engine Company, founded in 1864 (catalogue numbers WYL1771), as well

as many records relating to the establishment of the railways in Leeds and how the railway companies were run. The West Yorkshire Transport Executive Records (reference C181) cover more than a century of history from the 1870s and include staff records, photographs, wage books, copies of *Tramway and Railway World* and engineers' diaries. The collection comprises more than 4,000 items and covers Leeds, Bradford, Halifax and Huddersfield.

The office also has a large collection of documents relating to Middleton Colliery, which can be accessed via either the paper or online catalogue. These include maps, photographs, ledgers, journals and surveys dating back to 1762.

Leeds Local & Family History Library
As well as being home to dozens of volumes which cover the history of industry, engineering and the railways in Leeds, Leeds Local & Family History Library has maps and plans which cover the development of different sections of railway track and trade directories showing which businesses came and went as heavy industry progressed in the city.

Leeds Museums
The Leeds Museums have large holdings relating to trade and industry in Leeds, and the collections are particularly strong on textiles, engineering and printing, with well-known Leeds firms well represented, including Vickers PLC, Burtons, Kirkstall Forge, Hunslet Engine Company and John Fowler & Co. Not all material is on display at any one time and so the best course of action if you're interested in a particular industry or company is to contact the Leeds Museums Discovery Centre (tel.: 0113 378 2100; website: http://bit.ly/myleedsdiscovery).

Online information
Cleveland Family History Society has transcribed the 1853 Leeds Northern Railway Survey (http://www.clevelandfhs.org.uk/Leeds%20Northern.htm) which is available free of charge Here, staff members are listed along with their job title and salary.

The National Archives has a useful online guide to tracing railway ancestors (http://bit.ly/myleedsnarch) and the Search Engine library at the National Railway Museum in York has information on research that you can carry out at the museum if you have an ancestor who worked on the railways (http://www.nrm.org.uk/ResearchAndArchive/about.aspx).

Life on the Great Estates
Despite the urban environment of Leeds, the city did (and still does) have a number of mansion houses and surrounding estates. The most prominent of these are Lotherton Hall, Temple Newsam and Harewood House.

Lotherton Hall
The records for Lotherton Hall are kept at WYAS Leeds under reference WYL115. An online search of the WYAS catalogue will give you an overview of what aspect of this material you might like to explore. If you ancestor worked here or supplied goods to the estate, you may well find something of interest. The material includes information relating to tenants on the Gascoigne land, including leases and releases, surrender of terms, rental agreements, land surveys, railway plans and tenancy agreements.

There is also material relating to the Gascoigne family themselves, including a history, pedigrees of individual members in the nineteenth century, a diary of Sir Edward Gascoigne (from 1721 and 1726 to 1736), materials for a history of the family (from the eighteenth century) and Gascoigne accounts for coal mines in the area, mainly from the seventeenth century. There are also plans of the hall and its gardens.
Lotherton Hall, Aberford Leeds LS25 3EB; tel.: 0113 281 3259; website: www.leeds.gov.uk/museumsandgalleries/Pages/Lotherton-Hall.aspx

Harewood House
Harewood House was the property of the Lascelles family, whose wealth came from the sugar trade, and more controversially, the slave trade. The house regularly holds 'below stairs' exhibitions which show what life was like for those who worked for the family.

The house's archives are held by the Harewood House Trust and

The Great Houses of Leeds were a stark contrast to the back-to-back terraces many of our ancestors would have inhabited. © Tuck DB Postcards

the archive comprises some twenty-four boxes of papers from the eighteenth to twentieth centuries. There are photographs, cards, postcards, family papers, plans and election material which relates to Henry Lascelles's election campaign of 1807.
Harewood House, Leeds LS17 9LG; tel.: 0113 218 1010; email: info@harewood.org; website: www.harewood.org

Temple Newsam
WYAS Leeds holds the Temple Newsam collection (WYL100) which covers almost seven centuries – from 1271 to 1936. This important collection includes medieval records from the manor of Temple Newsam, maps and plans, day books, information on various families connected with the estate including the Scarboroughs, Skeltons and Hoptons, as well as papers relating to the Ingram

family, Viscounts Irwin, the later Wood family, and the Viscounts and Earls of Halifax. There are also inventories of household goods, schedules of deeds and stewards' papers. The Borthwick Institute at York (www.york.ac.uk/borthwick) also has information on the three years (1915–17) when the mansion acted as a military hospital in the First World War.
Temple Newsam, Temple Newsam Road, Leeds LS15 0EA; tel.: 0113 336 7560; website: http://bit.ly/myleedstn

Resources Relevant to All Leeds Trades
Many resources which are helpful in researching everyday life in Leeds, education, health and leisure time are also useful for finding out more about trade and industry in the city. Trade directories and local newspapers can be a good source of information about the prosperity (or otherwise) of a company or industry and if you search these records around the anniversary date of the founding of a particular firm, you may find information on celebratory events or awards.

If you'd like to see some pictorial source material, both the Leodis website and the Yorkshire Film Archive are of great interest. Leodis is strong on photographs of business premises, which you can search by company name or building name, whilst the Yorkshire Film Archive is useful for more recent history, with films of Middleton Railway locomotives, a documentary on the Burton suit factory from the 1950s, 1930s films charting the construction and opening of Lewis's department store and films showing the brewing process.

Chapter 4

STREET LIFE

From a small settlement on the banks of the River Aire to one of northern England's largest cities with a population of over 750,000 people, life in Leeds has changed greatly over the centuries. As Leeds grew in terms of population and area, it also shifted from a way of living focused on the river, through to a market town centred around Briggate, an increasingly wealthy Georgian town, and finally entering the industrial era with a concentration of industry. This saw the middle classes move out of the centre of town as industrial workers moved into Leeds in their thousands. These workers would be forced to take accommodation where they could find it, whilst prosperous suburbs began to emerge in Headingley and beyond for those who had the desire and the money to escape inner-city living.

In this chapter we begin by exploring how you can find out where in Leeds your ancestors lived, how to find out more about the house and the area in which it stood, and finally we take a look at local facilities, as we explore shopping in the city, from the earliest food markets through to the grand arcades of the Victorian era.

As we saw in Chapter 2, life in Leeds began on the banks of the River Aire and in the earliest years, accommodation was generally found close to where the main industries were located. As the textile industry grew up south of the river, so too did the districts of Armley, Hunslet and surrounding areas. Later on, the engineering and railway industries grew and prospered to the south and east of the town, bringing a growth in population to areas such as Cross Gates and Middleton.

With the huge growth in population at the time of the Industrial Revolution, incomers were often forced to take what accommodation they could find, leading to a growth in slum areas close to the city centre, with the squeeze on resources being heightened as successive waves of immigrants entered Leeds. Unscrupulous builders and landlords capitalised on the need for housing by building and renting back to back houses into which were squeezed large numbers of tenants, many of whom were forced to share toilet and washing facilities.

The Victorian age was one of great contrasts and as more and more workers packed into the centre of town, those wealthy enough to want to escape the grime and pollution began to head to suburbs north of Leeds, such as Roundhay, Chapeltown and Headingley. Here could be found large houses in spacious gardens, a far cry from the slums which were the lot of so many incomers.

By 1918, over 70 per cent of the city's houses were back to back properties. Although these houses may have looked almost identical,

A row of back-to-back terraces which typify the housing that became known as the 'Leeds look'.

Street Life

The Quarry Hills estate comprised almost 1,000 flats. © Tuck DB Postcards

a family's status could be demonstrated through the possession of a coveted 'through terrace', an end property with a yard at the side or even a bathroom in the attic. The low interest rates of the 1930s which followed the Great Depression brought about a boom in private house building, which began to creep out towards the suburbs.

A slum clearance began in the five years leading up to the Second World War, focusing particularly on York Road, the streets east of the markets and parts of Burmantofts. New council estates were built at Middleton and Gipton to house those moved from their demolished homes, and work also began on the famous Quarry Hill flats, a short-lived social experiment in high-rise living. The housing scheme at Quarry Hill comprised some 938 flats in buildings between four and eight storeys high. These were followed by more estates at Seacroft, Whinmoor and Swarcliffe, with the Queen 'opening' the settlement of Seacroft in 1965.

Back in the present day, the housing market has changed once more and nowadays, with the decline in heavy industry, both the suburbs and the city centre are seen as desirable places to live, with new apartment blocks standing on the sites of former factories and mills.

How to Find Out More about Where Your Ancestors Lived
There are several ways to find out where your ancestors lived and whether you manage to pinpoint their exact house, the street where they lived or even just the district, this needn't be the end of the story.

With a little extra research you can find out about the type of house in which your ancestor lived, even if it no longer exists. You may be lucky enough to discover an old photo of the house and we'll also explore how you can find out about the character of the street – what the neighbours did for a living, what local facilities would have existed when your ancestor lived there and how the district changed and grew over the years.

A great source of photographic evidence for both houses and streets is the Leodis website (www.leodis.org, see Chapter 9 for full details of the site). Here, you can search by street or district name (or other keyword) and there are also several photographic tours of the city including the centre, Morley, Briggate and Albion Place. Each image has background information; some have comments from other site users, and you can also order a print of the image.

Title deeds
One of the main sources for house history is actually held outside of Leeds, at the Registry of Deeds, West Yorkshire Archives Service in Wakefield. This registry is one of only two such offices in the country, and also holds of the majority of electoral and probate records for the district.

The deeds held at the registry comprise several million papers, dating from 1704 through to 1970, when the registry closed. These deeds are covered in more detail later in this chapter and if your ancestor registered a deed, you can uncover information on the type

Street Life

of property they owned, their occupation, other assets they held and businesses that belonged to them.

Until later in the twentieth century, registering the purchase of a property was a voluntary process. Title deeds are a collection of legal documents which relate to the past transfers of a property and their existence is a matter of chance – you may find only fifteen years' worth of records, or papers going back centuries which could include wills, manorial records and mortgages. The information that you find will give you the name of the vendor and purchaser, a date of sale, a description of the property and its price.

Council records
Council records are a useful resource and often overlooked because they rarely contain the names of anyone outside council employment. Nevertheless, they contain invaluable records of city life at a given point in time and because council reports were produced at least annually, it is easy to track changes in population, housing trends and even the health of the population.

Leeds L&FHL has a large selection of annual reports and a randomly selected report for 1914 to 1915 is a good example of how useful these records can be. The report has pages of statistics relating to life in Leeds at the start of First World War including the number of empty properties: 2,313 in 1915, compared to 7,144 four years earlier. The names of those council staff and workmen who had joined the armed forces (twenty-eight in total) are listed, along with their regiment, and a comment that 'owing to the war the work of both the office and the outside staff has been greatly disorganised'.

The changing nature of the city is reflected in a section of the report concerning 'unhealthy areas', which reports that some 105 houses in Quarry Hill had been demolished during the period March 1914 to March 1915. Some twenty years later, the area would become the home of the pioneering building scheme when Karl Marx-Hof-style flats were built by the Council. These had a life of just forty years and were demolished in 1978.

Another picture of a city at war within the same document is provided through a report that the Leeds Art Gallery had been given up as temporary accommodation for 300 Belgian refugees, with meals served in the sculpture gallery, the central hall converted to a playroom for the children, and separate men's and women's dormitories in smaller rooms. It was noted that 'absolutely no damage was done either to the works of art or to the building'.

Tracing the history of a house

When tracing the history of a house and its relative age compared to other houses in the same area, remember that, broadly speaking, older houses tend to be nearer to the town centre (as this is where the settlement usually began) with newer houses in the outlying areas and suburbs.

Before you begin your search, it is important to realise that records created for the construction of a property are few and far between so you'll largely be exploring records which were originally created for other purposes (such as trade directories) to find out more about the house and street you're interested in. You can download a property research guide from WYAS (http://bit.ly/myleedswyasproperty).

Rather than trying to trace a particular house through its building methods, it is easier and more interesting instead to trace its occupants back through the years, perhaps discovering who lived in the house before your ancestors, and what trades the various family members were involved in.

To begin with, you'll need to identify which parish the house was in – this should usually be marked on an Ordnance Survey map – both WYAS Leeds and Leeds L&FHL have large map collections. This will be a huge help in knowing which set of records you'll need to use as you work.

Once you've decided which property you'd like to trace, perhaps a house you've identified from a census as being one in which your ancestors lived, try to locate that property on the newest Ordnance Survey map that you can find and then work backwards using older maps. In doing so, you can not only trace when the house you're researching first appeared, but can also watch the surrounding area

Street Life

change around the house, perhaps as shops, churches and public buildings came and went.

Do bear in mind, however, that property names and numbers can change over time, so if you think you've traced a property back to its origins through OS maps, do check an older map just in case the property is even older than the 1840s, when the first OS maps were produced.

Tithe maps are another useful source and can be found at Leeds L&FHL and online (http://www.tracksintime.wyjs.org.uk). When church tithes changed to an annual tithe in 1840, a map was produced showing different parishes divided into numbered portions. These numbers relate to an accompanying tithe apportionment which gives the amount of land, plus information on its owners. The apportionment usually also has a description of the land and its state of cultivation.

Rate books are another resource, showing when an area was first rated. You can use these to search back over the years to see when a property was first built and who lived there during its history. You can then follow these occupants on censuses through to 1911, which is the most recently available census. When using censuses, do be aware that house numbers were not always recorded by the census enumerators; sometimes a single dash of a pen indicated the end of one property and the start of another one. Also, if a house was unoccupied at the time of a particular census, it won't be listed, no matter how old it is.

Electoral registers and street directories can also help to fill in the gaps between the censuses. Electoral registers (at WYAS Leeds and Leeds L&FHL) give both street names and house numbers for those householders eligible to vote. Electoral registers have been required practice since 1832 but it wasn't until 1918 that most men had the right to vote, followed by women over 21 in 1928.

The Registry of Deeds

Although obviously the Wakefield branch of WYAS holds less Leeds-related material than WYAS Leeds, it is still an important resource as it is home to the Registry of Deeds and also the headquarters of the West Yorkshire Archive Service. The Registry of Deeds is an important collection for anyone interested in tracing the history of a house or other property, and is one of only two such collections in the UK.

The West Riding Registry of Deeds (http://bit.ly/myleedsregistry) began in 1704. Its records, held at Wakefield WYAS, contain several million deeds from then until 1970, when the registry closed. Researchers in West Yorkshire are fortunate in that, unlike most of the rest of the country, millions of deeds relating to the area have survived. These can provide information about an individual or family, including the type of property they owned, their occupation, other assets they held and any businesses that belonged to them. The summaries of deeds held at Wakefield cover farms, houses, inns, shops and factories.

A deed is the title of ownership for a property and was drawn up to accompany the transaction of a sale of property between two parties. However, because it wasn't a legal requirement until 1970 for deeds to be registered, not all transactions were recorded.

The deed summaries are called memorials and contain the main details from the property deed. They are indexed by name and place and held in bound volumes. To use the registry, you need the name of the owner of the property. As well as listing previous deeds, tenants and sometimes former tenants, many deeds also recite previous deeds, going back over several generations.

The deeds often give interesting descriptions of the property involved in the transaction. If you are able to find several deeds for the same building, it will be possible to compare the documents and see how the property changed and evolved.

Shopping

Since medieval times when a market was held close to the River Aire, Leeds has been a centre for trading. Over the years, the first few temporary stalls were transformed into permanent markets, with shops, arcades and department stores developing as the town grew and prospered. However, our ancestors weren't only restricted to shopping in the town centre; outlying areas have long had their own

Street Life

Briggate, one of the city's oldest shopping streets. © Tuck DB Postcards

independent markets and later, corner shops, which thrived in the busy streets, offering goods for sale outside of traditional shopping hours.

In this section, we take a look at how to find out more about how and where our ancestors would have shopped in the past. Maybe you have an ancestor who was employed in the retail trade or perhaps you'd just like to find out more about what goods were available and where in Leeds. Through documentary evidence, photos and even film, you can explore the retail side of life in the city over the decades.

Markets

No study of the shopping scene in Leeds would be complete without a history of the markets of Leeds. From small beginnings with informal stalls on Leeds Bridge and surrounding streets, to the high-value trading carried out at the cloth halls and domestic shopping at the city markets, markets have a rich history in Leeds.

The earliest recorded market was at Briggate in 1207 but the heyday of the market was in the Victorian era, when Leeds was home to Central Market and South Market, with the magnificent Kirkgate Market which began as an open-air collection of stalls at the start of the nineteenth century. The first covered Kirkgate Market began in the 1850s, inspired by the grand design of the Crystal Palace in London. By the end of the nineteenth century, it was the biggest indoor market in Europe.

A grand new entrance was unveiled in 1904, although this was not without controversy, with some stallholders being given just a week's notice to move out of the building before work on the market began in 1901. The market continued to trade through the two World Wars and, despite damage from a severe fire in 1975, continues to this day, welcoming around 100,000 shoppers each week.

Although Kirkgate is the city's best known market, there have been others, including South Market on Meadow Lane and Central Market on Duncan Street, both of which were built in the 1820s. In fact, in the first half of the nineteenth century, five different markets were built, including Kirkgate. In 1875, the Leeds New Market was built. This was a roofed market which specialised in food, particularly meat and fish. There was also the famous Corn Exchange which opened in 1864 and acted as a large indoor centre for trade in grain.

Market records
Both WYAS Leeds and Leeds L&FHL hold publications devoted to the history of markets in Leeds. WYAS Leeds archive material includes market byelaws, photos, rental ledgers from the late 1800s to the 1960s, meat market and abattoir wage books, and books of press cuttings from 1945 to 1983.

The Brotherton Library at Leeds also holds papers relating to the White Cloth Hall from the period 1749 to 1847, including documents relating to the decision to build the third White Cloth Hall, registers of those who held stands, documents relating to the possibility of selling the hall, and the creation of the fourth Cloth Hall on King

Street. The third White Cloth Hall, which stood behind the present-day Corn Exchange, was Europe's most important marketplace for undyed cloth in the eighteenth century through until 1865. It was built to replace two former Cloth Halls (on Kirkgate and in Hunslet respectively) in 1775, with a fourth Cloth Hall being built in 1865 after the Third Hall would have been sliced in two with the coming of the railways.

You can also search local newspapers for references to the creation and development of markets in the city. Both advertisements and news reports show what life would have been like for traders and shoppers at a particular point in time. For example, a 'shocking occurrence' made a London paper named *The Era* on 31 May 1857, when it was reported that James Freeman, a 27-year-old 'jobbing hand' was sitting on a boiler at Kirkgate Market which was being heated to boil crabs. He unfortunately 'dropped off into a doze' and fell into the pan of boiling water. He was taken out by the men around him and conveyed to Leeds Infirmary, where he sadly died. Local newspapers contain regular reports on market traders which cover thefts from the stalls, bankruptcies, broken partnerships and receiving orders.

A case of Richard Robinson charged with obtaining cabbages under false pretences is one such example; amusing to modern eyes but a serious offence in 1898, when the *Nottinghamshire Guardian* reported on 8 October that the unfortunate Mr Robinson had appeared before Boston magistrates after being accused by farmer William Titman of taking the cabbages without giving payment. A week later, further evidence was presented by Mr Titman and, reported the paper again, Mr Robinson was committed for trial at the Quarter Sessions and was granted bail.

Shopping arcades
Leeds is famed for its shopping arcades and many of the most famous examples stand upon land which was once home to the medieval plots of bygone Leeds residents, on streets such as Briggate.

Thorntons Arcade is the oldest shopping arcade in the city and was opened in 1878. It was named after Charles Thornton, owner of the nearby Old White Swan Inn and City Varieties. The arcade is three storeys high and a key feature was a William Potts & Sons clock specially designed, with life-size figures.

Next came the Grand Arcade, opened in 1897 by the New Briggate Arcade Company and named after the nearby Grand Theatre. With its glass roof and arched windows, it offered a light and spacious all-weather shopping experience which must have been a marvel for those used to shopping in markets and corner shops. WYAS Leeds holds the records of the New Briggate Arcade Company, which run from 1720 to 1934 and comprise five boxes of documents which are available on open access although largely uncatalogued.

In 1889, Queens Arcade was opened by Edward Clark of London. At four storeys high and incorporating a grand hotel, this was

The grandeur of County Arcade. © Tuck D B Postcards

shopping at its finest. It was enlarged in 1895. County Arcade was built in 1900 by Frank Matcham on the site of an old meat market. With its marble floors and eye-catching masonry, it was a far cry from the trading post which it replaced.

You can see examples of different arcades and markets on the Leodis website (www.leodis.net). You can also check local newspapers around the date that each arcade was opened, or via a catalogue search under the name of the arcade, for details such as opening offers, stallholders, goods for sale and opening times.

Street and trade directories will also list the shops within an arcade, allowing you to build up a picture of which traders came and went over the years. These same resources can also be used to find out more about department stores and both chain stores and independent businesses.

The Headrow

Although much of Leeds grew up as the town grew in size and new industries developed, one of the main streets of Leeds was deliberately planned to bring some open space and order to an area of town known for its overcrowded nature.

Nowadays, The Headrow is a busy street upon which stand the Town Hall, City Library, Art Gallery and numerous shops and businesses. This area was originally known as the Head Row and comprised a row of houses which were literally at the head of the town; these buildings marked the most northerly part of Leeds. There was an upper and lower Head Row, both of which appear on the earliest known map of Leeds, which dates to 1560.

Over the years, the roads leading off the Head Row, as on other streets such as Briggate, had become a warren of small overcrowded buildings and dirty yards. A horse fair in the Upper Head Row and a cattle market at the lower end of the street added to the noise and filth.

After the cholera outbreaks of the 1830s, the authorities began to realise that open spaces and paved streets were desirable to try to prevent further outbreaks of the disease. As early as 1834 and writing in *Suggestions for the Improvements of our Towns and Cities,* author TS

Maslen suggested that: 'At some future time a great thoroughfare will be found to be necessary from east to west in the northern part of Leeds and it would be wise to begin early and provide a grand wide street for that purpose.'

In 1924, alderman Charles Lupton put forward a plan for this new east to west road which would cost £500,000 to create. Work on The Headrow was delayed by two years because of problems with land ownership but it was complete in the early 1930s, with the entire northern side of the road rebuilt by famed architect Sir Reginald Blomfield. In 1937, the Headrow Garden was opened and the war memorial was moved from its location on City Square to stand here, close to the grand new buildings and the Town Hall.

The oldest known map of Leeds dates to 1560.

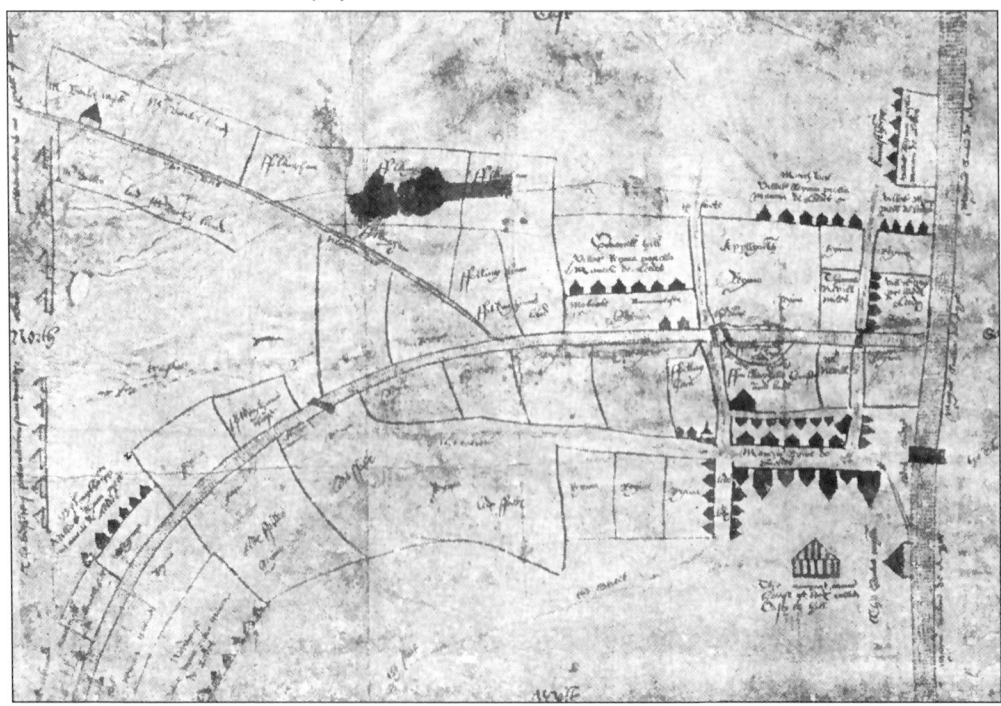

Street Life

The Headrow.

Shopping Archive Resources
From small market stalls to huge department stalls, for centuries Leeds shoppers have had a wealth of shopping choices within the streets of the town. Whether you're hoping to find out more about what shops and markets your ancestor might have visited, or would like to find out more about an ancestor's place of work, this section explores the main retail collections available to researchers.

Marks & Spencer Company Archives
From small beginnings as a penny store in Leeds Market, Marks & Spencer's has become a globally known name. In the company's centenary year of 1984, it was decided to create an archive, which is based in Leeds. This also has a useful website (http://marksintime.marksandspencer.com) which can help you identify themes to help with your research.

Whether you have an ancestor who worked for Marks & Spencer's, would simply like to find out more about how shopping tastes have changed over the years, or trace the history of a particular store, there's plenty of information to explore. Each of the themes listed on the site has a search facility. So, for example, the store history section allows you to choose the keyword 'Leeds' which returns more than 130 records. Among the treasures available to view are a photo album of the first Leeds store from 1851 through to 1981; training bulletins from the 1940s; and Christmas merchandise from the city centre shop in the 1920s.

The reading room is located at the University of Leeds and you'll need to book at least a day in advance of your visit. Once there, you can explore the archive catalogue and photos, and staff are available to help with initial queries. Although the archive doesn't hold personnel records or wage books, there are quite a few avenues for research. Of particular interest for tracing ancestors at the company, or finding out what life was like there, are employee records such as conditions of employment and employee regulations, employee uniforms, photos from staff and social events and merchandise from over the years.

The archive also has copies of *Sparks*, the company's newsletter, for the years 1934 to 1984. Among the potential leads here are sports and social club news, long service news, obituaries and letters. Also available for study are copies of *St Michael's News* (for 1953 to 1999) which include details of new store openings and information on individual stores.

Archive material also shows the company's contribution to the war effort, with copies of the store's Second World War *Forces Bulletin* magazine for M&S colleagues fighting on the Front; M&S experts' guidance on producing utility clothing and photographs of the café bars set up in store to provide the public with a break from the strictures of food rationing.

Leeds Industrial Co-operative Society
The Co-operative in Leeds had its headquarters on Albion Street, where the company owned two blocks of buildings covering various

retail departments, under the banner 'Join the Co-operative Society – Save as you Spend'. The society was founded in 1847 at a time when applications for Poor Relief in Leeds had reached over 2,000 per year. Thousands of townspeople were visiting soup kitchens each week and many families struggling to survive on meagre wages.

Members were encouraged to pay in a penny per week in order to allow the society to purchase a mill to supply flour to the needy public at a reasonable price. From small beginnings with the building of the People's Mill, by the 1860s, the Leeds Industrial Co-operative Society had become the largest Co-operative Society in the UK. The successful society diversified into both food and non-food goods and became a familiar name in the city centre and suburbs.

The WYAS Leeds records cover the years 1847 to 2007 and include registers of attendees at the regular meetings, copies of the society's newsletters, photos of staff members (from the early twentieth century to the 1970s), books of press cuttings from 1903 to 1972, and photos of various early co-operative industries, including a laundry, bakers and wheelwrights. There are also records for the Leeds District Cooperative Womens' Guild and the Chapel Allerton & Central Cooperative Womens' Guild.

The Co-operative produced a magazine for shoppers from the 1940s, called *The Record* which can be viewed at Leeds Local Studies Library (shelf mark L334.5 L517). The 'moderns' section aimed at teenagers is particularly interesting in identifying incoming trends, and there are also tips on food and cooking, showing what foods and cooking styles were in fashion.

Chapter 5

EDUCATION

The story of education in Leeds is linked firmly to the growth of the city and its industries. The population of Leeds at the start of the nineteenth century was some 53,000 and by 1841, there were over 100 woollen mills with 10,000 employees and some thirty flax-spinning mills employing 5,000 people. The population was 157,000 – almost triple that of forty years earlier. Most industry was south of the river at Hunslet and Holbeck, where overcrowded terracing grew up.

At the start of the nineteenth century, the only education available to children of working-class families was a Sunday school or a dame school – an establishment which basically fulfilled the role of a childminder for working parents. By the 1830s, Leeds had a National School, a Royal Lancastrian School (mainly for the middle classes) and four Wesleyan Schools. For the less well off, there was a charity school in Mark Lane and a small number of ragged schools which were paid for by public subscription, in order to keep vagrant children off the streets (and stop the petty crimes they committed).

The 1864 and 1867 Factory Acts had ruled that children who worked outside of the textile trade had to attend school. But it was the 1870 Elementary Education Act which brought in schooling for the masses and ushered in a new era of school building.

Within just a few months of the passing of the 1870 Act, it became clear that the newly elected Leeds School Board had plenty of work ahead of it. A government report of 1869 by Joshua Fitch had concluded that many of the working-class children were enduring a 'totally inadequate' education system. Indeed, a census in 1871 revealed that, under the terms of the 1870 Education Act, some 58,000 children would need to be educated – only 12,000 of whom were currently receiving a suitable education.

The Elementary Education Act ushered in a new age of school building.

The Leeds School Board proposed a design competition for the new schools and architects were invited to submit school designs, to win prizes of £50 and £25 – plus the ensuing commissions of designing Leeds schools. Some fifty-two designs were received and the winners were George Carson of Leeds and Alexander & Henman of Stockton & Middlesbrough. Carson was commissioned to design the city's first Board School, in Beverley Street, whilst Alexander & Henman designed a school on Burley Road.

The Education Act of 1902 effectively abolished school boards and councils took over as local education authorities. The year before, the leaving age had been raised from 11 to 12. By 1918, all pupils had to stay at school until at least the age of 14.

The board existed between 1870 and 1903 and was created

following the Elementary Education Act of 1870. Board members were elected by the rate payers and the Board used its income to build and run schools and to subsidise church schools where necessary. School attendance was also monitored.

Once the City Council had taken over education, new schools were built on housing estates including Crossgates and Meanwood, where large populations could benefit from them. The council also began to take over secondary schools which had been privately run. Leeds Council took over the Leeds Boys' and Girls' Modern schools in 1907 and the West Leeds High School opened in Armley in 1907 for 600 children. But even in the mid-1920s, there were only fourteen secondary schools in the whole city, and 121 primary schools. With 67,000 children in primary education at this time, only 6,300 went on to pursue a secondary education to age 14 or beyond.

By 1925, the city had over forty technical evening schools which were educating almost 10,000 students in evening classes. Many people who worked during the day took part in classes which taught skills either to further their career (subjects such as science and engineering) or leisure interests (cookery and sewing).

In the early twentieth century, secondary schools were fee paying, with the exception of those few pupils who won a scholarship and whose parents were prepared to forego their potential household income by allowing them to stay on and attend secondary school.

Leeds Grammar School
The first mention of what would become Leeds Grammar School was made in 1341, however the school was founded in 1552 by Reverend William Sheafield who left £14 13s 6d in his will to provide education for the children of the town. The first school house was in the centre of town, most likely in the Calls area, and moved to Headingley Lane at the end of the sixteenth century. In 1624, benefactor John Harrison moved the school to a 'pleasant field' at New Briggate, where the present Leeds Grand Theatre stands. There was a further move in 1857, away from the growing industry of the town, to Woodhouse Moor (near the current university) and finally, in the 1990s, to Alwoodley, five miles north of the city.

The chapel at Leeds Grammar School. © Tim Green

Evening Classes

No matter how long they stayed on at school, your ancestor may well have attended evening classes, either to improve their job prospects or to pursue a hobby with like-minded people. Many interest-orientated societies have their roots in the Victorian age – Leeds Photographic Society was founded in 1852, Leeds Astronomical Society in 1859 and the Leeds Art Club in 1893. It wasn't all about indoor activities either. Potternewton Club had almost 150 members at the end of the nineteenth century who would regularly enjoy bike rides to the east coast. Many amateur and hobby societies have deposited their archives at WYAS over the years but those that are still in existence may still hold their own archive material. The activities of local societies also sometimes appear in the pages of local newspapers, particularly around the time of landmark anniversaries.

One way to get on within a trade or profession was to attend evening classes.

How to Find Out about Your Ancestor's Schooling

So how can you find out what school your ancestor might have attended? If you know their address, the best place to start is a street directory for the year nearest to the age they would have started

Education

Pupils at Brudenell School in 1949. The school was demolished in the 1990s.

school. Leeds L&FHL has a large collection and these books list the schools in the city, often with the names of staff members and the principal.

Once you've found the nearest few schools to where your ancestor lived, it is a matter of locating the records for those schools and trying your luck from there. If a school still exists, it may still hold its own records and a call to the school office should point you in the right direction. If it is a school no longer in existence, try a search on the Access to Archives website (http://apps.national archives.gov.uk/a2a) or the WYAS site (http://www.archives.wyjs.org.uk) archive catalogue.

Once you've narrowed down your search, what records will help you find out more? First of all, any school records newer than a century old may well be subject to a closure period or restricted viewing, particularly 'sensitive' information such as punishment books. The following section has some ideas on where to begin your research.

Education Records

Records at WYAS Leeds
WYAS Leeds has a large collection of school records, which can be searched via a paper catalogue at the archive office or on the online catalogue.

Log books are a good source of information for what life was like at a particular school, or during a particular period of time. These books were kept by the head of a school (in a similar way to a diary) and recorded landmark events in the school year, visitors to the school, the appointment of new teachers and the awarding of prizes, etc. Even if your family member isn't mentioned, you can get a flavour of what school life was like in a given period.

Dozens of individual schools are covered in the WYAS education catalogue, alongside wider ranging records for school boards and the city's education department. Schools in the records include Belle Isle, Beecroft, Benjamin Gott High School, Cross Gates, Garforth Barley Hill, Leeds Girls High School, Harehills Primary, Holt Park and

Education

Methley, as well as further flung areas in the Leeds Council education district such as Otley, Pudsey, Yeadon, Wetherby and Guiseley.

Within the paper catalogue, schools are catalogued in alphabetical order, with individual records for each school listed under that establishment. For example, Headingly Primary records cover the years 1882 to 2006 and records include log books (1882–1972), punishment books, visitor books, a souvenir handbook (1926), a history of the school, photo albums from the 1960s and admission registers for 1924 to 1944.

A log book for Blenheim Middle School covering the years 1873 to 1887 is a good example of what information such sources can reveal. It is a large bound book with an introduction which states that no entries are to be removed or altered once made, and that the principal teacher must write an entry at least once a week about the school's progress, illnesses and visits from managers. The principal teacher was also instructed to copy into the book the summary of the inspector's report after his annual visit to the school.

Such log books are essentially a diary of school life, as seen through the eyes of the headteacher. 'Latecoming prevails,' the head writes in an 1877 entry.

> I believe it is greatly the fault of the children. Many boys have had to remain in school after dismissal for not satisfactorily preparing their home lessons.

The book goes on to give a summary of the inspector's report which states that 'the boys prove that they have been intelligently taught'.

In 1879, the principal reports that that a holiday was given as the teachers had their annual excursion to Scarborough and York. And there were rewards for pupils too: 'The boys who were most attentive to lessons were allowed to attend the Baths.' But of course things could go wrong too, and here a pupil is mentioned by name – a fairly rare occurrence: 'W Boden sent a note complaining that his teacher struck him in the head with a slate.'

Leeds School Board and City Council education department records
Leeds WYAS has records of the Leeds School Board for 1858 to 1951,

as well as education department reports which include inspector's reports and school attendance returns.

The school board records are catalogued under reference LLT6 and include site and building records, school portfolios, records for industrial and special schools, school building accounts and scholarship accounts.

Education department records are filed under reference LC/ED and include books of press cuttings, school attendance committee returns, salary records, school site plans and governors' minutes. Material less than 100 years old may be subject to viewing restrictions and WYAS staff can advise on this.

Local newspapers

Local newspapers are a rich source of information on both pupils and staff at Leeds schools and colleges. Such establishments regularly sent through reports of examination results, new buildings or departments, school excursions and new appointments. And of course, the alumni of such establishments often moved far from Leeds, therefore an online newspaper service such as Nineteenth-Century British Newspapers (available online through Leeds Libraries – see more details in Chapter 9) allows you to search by both school name or by an individual's name. The collections include obituaries of former Leeds school pupils and teachers, you can follow their careers through university and the professions. The *Leeds Mercury* of 28 March 1835 carried the following notice: 'Mr John Haigh of Queen's College, Oxford, (formerly at the Leeds Grammar School) has been elected by the Provost and Fellows of that society, to one of the valuable exhibitions of the founding of Sir Francis Bridgeman.'

Leeds University Archive

Leeds University Archive preserves records relating to the history of Leeds University and its predecessor institutions including the Yorkshire College of Science. Records exist for staff, students and individuals with close associations to the university, along with photographs, maps and plans relating to the development of the site and its buildings and departments.

The archive catalogue is available at the archives (with paper

Education

finding aids) and online (http://bit.ly/myleedsuniversity), and both catalogues list over 8,000 records arranged into twelve sub-collections: academic & other services, administrative records, audio-visual collection, committee records, departmental records, objects, plans & drawings, personalia, photographic collection, published sources, staff records and student records.

Of most interest to anyone following the fortunes of an ancestor with connections to the university are staff records (1922–2003) and student records for 1879–2003. The photograph collections have individuals and groups, as well as building interior and exteriors. Material at the archives is available to researchers by prior appointment via the university library's Special Collections.

Trade directories

As an example of the amount of education information available in trade directories, the Leeds and District Trades Directory for 1902–3 (kept at Leeds L&FHL) has listings for academies, schools and teachers. There is an extended entry for the Berlitz School of Languages and Translation Bureau on Park Row, which offers 'native speakers and trial lessons free'. 'French, German and Spanish', continues the entry, are 'taught by the surest and most rapid methods'.

Also listed is the Leeds Institute of Science, Art & Literature on Cookridge Street which offered a library with lectures, a school of art, school of music, commercial evening school and boys' and girls' modern schools.

The Kelly's Directory for the same period is more comprehensive in its coverage of education in the city, with listings of over twenty private schools for boys and girls, many in suburbs such as Roundhay and Headingley. Also listed are twenty-six Leeds state schools, along with each school's address and the name of the headteacher. There are also commercial schools, a post office school of telegraphy (in City Square), the Wesleyan Methodist Theological College in Headingley and the St Joseph's Catholic Seminary on Seminary Street.

Chapter 6

MIGRATION AND POVERTY

For centuries Yorkshire had a reputation as being a place of plentiful employment and Leeds, the 'city of 1,000 trades' with its location between ports for the North Sea and ports offering access to the Americas, detained or delayed many a traveller who had been intending to journey from mainland Europe on to the Americas.

People travelled to Leeds from all over the world but, particularly in the nineteenth century, entered a labour market that was already saturated. Although immigrants were often able to settle in areas close to their kinsmen, these areas were frequently overcrowded with poor facilities.

In this chapter we look at how to find out what life was like for immigrant ancestors and for those who lived in poverty, as well as exploring resources which can shed light on these subjects.

Immigration
The first large wave of immigrants into England arrived from France and the Low Countries during the sixteenth century. Many of these people tended to stay around London, where work was plentiful and it wasn't until the nineteenth century, when Yorkshire became a strong player in the Industrial Revolution, that immigrants reached Leeds in any numbers.

The potato famine that began in Ireland in 1845 and the pogroms of the Russian Empire were just two of the big events that caused people to leave their homeland to begin a new life in England, moving to Yorkshire for work. The twentieth century saw further waves of immigration, triggered mainly by the two World Wars, bringing refugees from Eastern Europe. These were followed by immigrants from Commonwealth countries, eager to make the most

Migration and Poverty

The Industrial Revolution brought in thousands of immigrant families.

of the freedom of colonists to come and go as they wished. Many of those who arrived from Pakistan, India and Jamaica took employment in the textile mills of Leeds.

Census records

Census returns can be an excellent way to find out not only when immigrant ancestors arrived in an area but also to examine the ethnic makeup of an area. The first English census which is any use for family history purposes is the 1841 census but it is only from the 1851 census onwards that enumerators recorded where a person had been born; the 1841 census records only that a person originated from 'foreign parts'.

Lack of local knowledge often led immigrants to the worst areas of town.

Daddy, I'm Hungry.

Migration and Poverty

When you have found your ancestors on the census, take a look at the returns for the houses and streets around their address. This will allow you to build up a picture of what proportion of their neighbours came from the same country, what sort of occupations the neighbours followed and the number of people who lived in each house.

Immigrant areas were notorious for overcrowding, with incomers being forced, through lack of money or local knowledge, to take the poorest accommodation on offer, in the worst areas of Leeds.

Groups and societies

Generally speaking, once an immigrant arrived in Leeds, he or she would appear only on the same records as other Leeds residents, such as trade directories, censuses, voter lists, etc. However, one of the other ways in which you might be able to trace your ancestor's progress in the city is through any groups he or she might have belonged to, including religious organisations. Religion is covered in Chapter 7 and these records can include church magazines, newspaper reports of parades or commemorations, or church birth, marriage and burial records. Clubs for sports and hobbies are another resource to try, using local newspaper records for reports of meetings and events.

Immigrants often had a strong sense of identity with their home country, not only choosing to live close to others from the same country of origin, but also forming societies and organisations specifically for immigrants. Irish immigrants had the Irish Centre on York Road (which still exists) and its predecessors, the 'Irish Nash' on Briggate and an Irish centre close to Mount St Marys Church. Jewish societies are well represented too, with the Leeds Jewish Society, the Leeds Jewish Welfare Board and the Leeds Jewish Blind Society. As with other non-immigrant clubs and groups, records may have been handed to WYAS or could still be kept with the association concerned.

Oral history

Several projects have recorded the experiences of immigrants to the city and one of the most recent is Untold Stories (www.untoldstories.

co.uk) which explores the experiences of Irish immigrants. The website has photo collections on the history of Irish immigration, which show what life was like for new immigrants, how immigrants settled into life in Leeds and the experiences of modern-day Leeds citizens with Irish roots. The site also has a documentary film and suggestions for further reading.

Yorkshire Film Archive (www.yorkshirefilmarchive.com) has over a dozen films relating to immigrant life that you can watch online, including sports, religious and cultural events.

Poverty

The workhouse
That feared institution the workhouse, which is often imagined as a Victorian institution, actually opened in Leeds parish in 1638, located at the point where Lady Lane joins Vicar Lane, above The Headrow. This workhouse was short-lived, though, and by the early 1700s, the workhouse had become a charity school. For three years (from 1725 to 1728) the workhouse reopened but the harsh conditions caused unrest among the inmates and it closed its doors again, this time for another ten years when it reopened and was extended in 1740, with separate provision for 'lunatics'. Up to 200 inmates could be housed here and were managed by a body of overseers.

The coming of the Industrial Revolution and its attendant wave of immigrants put such pressure on the Leeds Workhouse that it was decided a new one should be built. This was designed by Elisha Blackhouse and William Perkins, who also worked on the Ripon Workhouse. The new Leeds Union Workhouse was completed in 1861 and was still undergoing extensions into the twentieth century. By now, a new Leeds Poor Law Union had come into being and this covered a huge area of around 110,000 people, including the suburbs of Headingley, Rounday and Seacroft. The workhouse later became part of the famous St James's Hospital.

Workhouse records are kept by WYAS Leeds and include records of administration and discharge for 1843–7, Guardians' Minutes for 1844 to 1930, an adoptions register for 1895 to 1948 and an inmates' register for 1784 to 1795. Whilst admission registers for the city are

Leeds Union Workhouse inmates. © Leeds Teaching Hospitals NHS Trust

few, a rich source of information that you can use instead are the board of guardian's admissions and letter books. These two resources deal with the point at which families or individuals were admitted to the workhouse. Even if you're not lucky enough to find an ancestor listed, these resources show the many different reasons why people ended up having to rely on the workhouse and the circumstances which led up to their admittance.

Workhouses covering the Leeds area are known to have existed at Armley, Chapel Allerton, Calverley with Farsley, Farnleyn, Gildersome, Holbeck, Horsforth, Hunslet, Leeds, Rothwell Wetherby and Wortley. Typical records include overseers' minutes, workhouse masters journals, rate books detailing the collection of the poor rate from rate payers in the parish.

Leeds voluntarily exempted itself from the New Poor Law, which meant that it was exempted from many of the Act's provisions, such as the need to provide all poor relief within the setting of the workhouse. However, from 1834 the Leeds guardians were appointed by the Poor Law Commissioners. They set up the Leeds Moral and Industrial Training Schools where boys were expected to work on tasks such as shoemaking to help earn their keep. The school was built between 1846 and 1848 at Beckett Street and the original building is now the Lincoln Wing of St James's Hospital. A new workhouse was created in 1858, along with an infirmary (now the Thackray Medical Museum).

Poor relief records at WYAS Leeds
Leeds WYAS has a large number of records relating to poor relief, from early documents such as settlement certificates, through to overseers' accounts and records of workhouse inmates.

Early poor relief in Leeds, as elsewhere in the country, tended to be administered as outdoor relief, whereby claimants were helped in their own homes. Each pauper was the responsibility of the parish where he or she had been born and so, if a pauper moved to a new parish, that parish would be keen to return that person to whence they had come, so as to ensure he or she didn't become a financial burden.

In order to claim relief, the claimant needed a settlement certificate, which was proof that he or she was entitled to receive relief from the parish in which they were settled. These were issued by overseers of the poor who carried out settlement examinations if there was any question about a person's entitlement to relief. If the person wasn't entitled to be in the parish, a removal order would be produced.

Beware of assuming that the parish named in the settlement certificate is the place where the person concerned was born, as there were exceptions and paupers could gain the right to claim relief if they had lived in the parish for a certain number of years, had served as an apprentice there or rented property within the area.

WYAS has a large number of settlement certificates and removal registers (from the eighteenth century through to 1901) relating to Yorkshire and these can be searched in the paper catalogue or online

Migration and Poverty

by the person's name or the name of the parish. Bastardy records held at the office cover the years 1844 to 1930.

The 1834 Poor Law Amendment Act curtailed outdoor relief and it was only the desperate who would claim relief by entering the workhouse. The parish as a unit of administration came to be replaced by the Poor Law Unions. A board of guardians for the township of Leeds was instituted in 1844 – the Leeds Union covered Leeds, Chapel Allerton, Headingley, Burley, Roundhay and Seacroft. The Bramley Union covered Armley, Bramley, Farnley, Gildersome and Wortley. In 1869 the Holbeck and Hunslet Unions were formed.

Workhouse records at WYAS Leeds

Workhouse admission and discharge books, held at WYAS Leeds, although not indexed by name, can hold a surprising amount of information, both on general life in the workhouse and the lives of individual members of staff or workhouse inmates.

The Leeds Workhouse Admissions and Discharge Book for 1843–7 is a volume which gives account of every pauper admitted into the workhouse, through until their discharge or death.

Each admission entry has the person's name, place of birth, parish they belonged to at the time of admittance, their occupation, marital status and, if a child, whether or not they are an orphan, deserted or bastard child. The entries continue with information on whether or not the person was able-bodied, details of any disability, whether they had been receiving relief, the cause of them seeking entry into the workhouse, religious persuasion and general observations on the person's condition at the time of admittance.

Discharge information can be enlightening, comments such as 'taken out by their brother', 'died', 'absented herself without leave', 'sent to Wakefield Asylum' give a flavour of the comments. Remarks on the condition of inhabitants range from 'clean, decent' to 'cannot do with having to pay for housing' and 'in a low despondent state of mind and helpless'. Conditions which would now be identified as possible mental health issues were not dealt with as such.

WYAS Leeds also has books of poor law letters, including records for the Hunslet and Leeds Unions. As an example, a masters' book

THE POET BETWEEN HIS TWO DEBORAHS

Workhouse letter books often give vivid accounts of workhouse life

Migration and Poverty

for Leeds covering June through to August 1874 includes letters from inmates, families, tradespeople and workhouse staff. The master's report pleads with staff to stop allowing inmates to go to bed wearing their clothes on Sunday afternoons, as the practice is leaving the dormitories in a 'dirty and filthy condition'.

In other letters, inmates ask for leave of absence. Because these letters aren't indexed by name, it is a matter of exploring the records and seeing what you find. And even if an ancestor isn't named, the records give a flavour of workhouse life. Many of the letters from inmates are written in an educated hand with perfect grammar, proof perhaps that it could be sheer bad luck that brought a family to the workhouse.

Reports on individual inmates found within the letter books again name individuals and if you are lucky enough to find an ancestor mentioned, there can be plenty of information on the person's character and fate. However, you may be surprised at the lack of compassion shown in the reports: 'Dishonest, dirty, idle and untruthful', 'dishonest, dirty, idle and bad in every way', 'works in a factory and is a very wild, bad girl' and poignantly: 'Imbecile, no improvements'.

There are glimmers of the less ordinary too, including a master's report on a lady visitor who smuggled a bottle of whisky to one of the visitors: 'the master has kept the same in his custody until the decision of the board'.

Also of interest are records from tradespeople who were providing goods to the workhouse, or advertising their wares. In the 1874 letterbook for Hunslet Union is a leaflet from the Continental and Colonial Traders who were advertising their Californian beef and Sydney mutton for 5¾d and 5¼d respectively, presumably for the workhouse master to purchase for the inmates.

Local newspapers

Local newspapers are worth checking if you believe you had an ancestor who spent time in one of the Leeds workhouses. Nineteenth-century newspapers regularly ran advertisements relating to workhouse inmates who had absconded. These make for poignant reading and often include a detailed physical description, as in this excerpt from the *Leeds Mercury* on 11 October 1817:

> Absconded and left his family chargeable to the township of Leeds: George Blackburn by trade a cabinet maker, stands about 5 feet 7.5 inches high black hair, hair a little bald, a tooth out and stout made. Had on when he left his family a bottle green coat, striped waistcoat and Kerseymere breeches.

The notice offers a reward of one guinea to whoever finds George and lodges him in 'any of his majesty's gaols'.

The workhouse in the census
The first you may know of an ancestor being in the workhouse could be if you find reference to them in a census. The 1881 census for Leeds Union Workhouse on Beckett Street lists both staff and inmates, with the institution headed up by workhouse overseer John Yabsley Avery (age 45) and his wife Emma Avery (age 44) who was the matron. Their two children Alfred and Kate are also listed, along with the master of the smallpox hospital (George Buxton) and the matron, Esther Buxton.

Next come the inmates, listed by name, occupation, age and place of birth. Looking at the list is a fascinating snapshot of workhouse life at this time – ages in the 1881 Leeds Union Workhouse inmate listing range from three months to inmates in their eighties, whilst occupations include a shoemaker, charwoman, painter, cart driver, rag sorter and seamstress – clearly almost anyone could fall on hard times.

Leed's Tradesmens Benevolent Institution
Established by a wealthy tea merchant in 1843, the Leeds' Tradesmens Benevolent Institution was originally created to save poor families from the workhouse and continues as a charity for the elderly today.

Although the records of Leeds Infirmary (which stands on the site of the city's workhouse) are held by WYAS Leeds, the majority of other archive material relating to hospitals, workhouses and asylums in Leeds are held by WYAS Wakefield, and some of this material is not on open access, due to the sensitive nature of some documents. However, staff at WYAS are always happy to advise.

Leeds Pious Uses Committee

Classed as one of the 'treasures' of the West Yorkshire Archive Service, the records of the Leeds Pious Uses Committee date back to 1621, when a committee of the vicar of Leeds and eleven prominent Leeds townspeople were chosen to act as trustees for the management for all of the charities in Leeds.

The committee acted on behalf of the Highways Estate, trying to improve town life for everyone, allowing streets or footpaths to be widened, improving the layout of certain areas of town and arranging for the repair or demolition of public buildings.

This collection also includes early records for the Free Grammar School (a forerunner of Leeds Grammar School) and Leeds Charity School, as the committee was also involved in arranging for the education of poor children. The collection can be explored at WYAS Leeds (LC01010) and covers the years 1664 to 1934.

Living conditions for the poor

Local history books, and contemporary books and magazines can give us a good idea about what life would have been like for those who lived in the poorest parts of town.

Writing in his paper 'The White Slaves of England', in *Pearsons Magazine*, R Sheracy said in the 1890s that the Jewish tailors he visited at the Jewish Tailors' Union in the Leylands

> all work on a daily wage and from 12 to 17 hours a day. Here may be seen in some filthy room in an old dilapidated factory in the Leylands, fifty people (men, women, boys and girls) all huddle together, sewing as though for dear life…
>
> The stench in the room, its uncleanliness, surpass description. The finished garments are lying pell mell on the floor in the filth and vermin.

Joseph Clayton of Hunslet, described in the census as a 'blanket raiser', spoke in *Hynoptic Leeds* in 1894:

the typical workman's house in Leeds has one living room with sink and taps for washing purposes, two bedrooms and an attic in which possibly is a bath. The bath is the redeeming point and the corporation should insist on it being built in every house.

The sinks and taps on the other hand are depressing in a sitting room and the atmosphere of the weekly wash not conducive to health of mind or body… our ashpits which adorn the street are the resting place for decayed vegetable matter and domestic refuse… in Leeds the jerry builder flourishes, crushing into a small space rows of these red brick kennels.

If you'd like to try to find out whether or not your ancestor lived in poor conditions, you can use a mixture of maps, street directories and old photographs to build up a picture of life in a particular street or district. The Leodis website has hundreds of photos of old streets. On maps it is a good rule of thumb that, the more closely packed into an area the streets and housing plots are, the poorer that area would have been.

Chapter 7

RELIGION

In this chapter we explore the history of religion in Leeds, from the earliest place of worship close to an ancient crossing place on the River Aire, through the height of non-conformity and on to non-Christian religions which became more visible as the population of the city grew and changed.

Because many religious groups have faced hostility or even persecution at some point in their history, their records have not always survived or were maybe never even kept in the first place. The Hardwick Act of 1754 stated that everyone except Jews or Quakers had to be married in the established church or face transportation from the country.

Understandably, such a stiff penalty meant that those who wished to go through a marriage ceremony for their own religion might not have wanted a record of the occasion to be kept for posterity. Many people opted to marry both in their own religion and to go through a Church of England ceremony for the sake of keeping to the law. This means that if you find a marriage of our ancestors in a Church of England parish register before 1837, it isn't safe to assume that they followed the beliefs of the established church.

Church of England
Christianity has been practised in Leeds for over 1,000 years, with the first worshippers settling beside the River Aire by the eighth century. Carved stone crosses have been found in the town dating to the tenth century; evidence of settled worship close to the river. The mother church of the Leeds area was St Peter's (now known as Leeds Parish Church or Leeds Minster) and this place of worship covered a large parish of over thirty miles, including villages as far afield as Headingley and Farnley.

TRINITY CHURCH.

Trinity Church, established in 1727.

The present-day Minster was consecrated in 1841, by Dr WF Hook, one of the greatest theologians of the Victorian era. He arrived in Leeds in 1838, at a time that the town's industries were fast developing, and realised that the small church which stood on the site of the present one was inadequate for a fast-growing population. He set plans in motion for a new place of worship that could seat 1,600 parishioners.

Religion

The new minster was by no means the only place of worship for those who followed the established church – St John's Church on New Briggate (the city's oldest church still in existence) had opened in 1634. Between 1700 and 1790, the population of Leeds quadrupled, bringing with it a new age of church and chapel building. In 1714, the vicar of Leeds, the mayor, three aldermen and Leeds historian Ralph Thoresby began to raise funds for a new church. They purchased land on Boar Lane but it would be six years before the foundations were laid for the building which would become Holy Trinity Church. The new church opened in 1727, serving a mainly wealthy group of worshippers, as parishioners had to rent the pews.

How to find Church of England records
As of Easter 2014, the old Diocese of Ripon and Leeds was dissolved and replaced by the Diocese of West Yorkshire and the Yorkshire Dales. Prior to civil registration, baptism, marriages and burial records can be found in parish records, some of which date back to the sixteenth century. WYAS Leeds holds microfiche copies for parishes which cover Leeds and surrounding areas, and many of these records are also available through Ancestry.

Although the Parochial Registers and Records Measure which was passed by the General Synod of the Church of England in 1978 recommended that parish records be deposited in local record offices, do be aware that not all such records were passed on and some are still held by individual churches.

WYAS's 'collections guide 1', available on the WYAS website (http://bit.ly/myleedscollect1) has a list of the different Leeds parishes, the collection reference number, the years which the baptism, marriage and death records cover, and which WYAS office holds those records.

Non-Conformism
Perhaps because of the distance of the city from the centre of power in Westminster, for centuries Leeds held a reputation as a centre for non-conformism. Early Methodist preachers found an eager audience for their sermons, although not everyone appreciated

Early preachers needed a strong will and a thick skin.

Religion

hearing about a religion other than that of the established church, as we shall see.

The nineteenth century was a boom period for those who wished to worship outside the established church and it was during this time that religions such as Methodism, the Quakers and Baptists flourished and gained recruits at the expense of the Church of England, which had been slow to respond to the huge growth in the population of Leeds.

WYAS Leeds has a helpful non-conformism research guide (http://bit.ly/myleedscollec2), which includes advice on how to find out whether an ancestor was a non-conformist, and where the various non-conformism records can be found. The records span the years 1646 to 1985. Some of these registers haven't yet been microfilmed and so have to be viewed in their original form at the relevant WYAS office, and such records are clearly highlighted in the guide. The data are organised in the same way as records for the established church, with the name of the church given, followed by denomination, collection reference, the relevant dates for the records held and an indication of which WYAS office holds those records.

Roman Catholicism

Yorkshire had a strong tradition of Catholicism during the years in which the faith was banned in England, although there were as few as fifty Roman Catholic families in Leeds after the Reformation. Red Hall at Roundhay and Middleton Hall in Ilkley, fifteen miles from Leeds, were recusant centres where the faith could be practised in secret. Following the Catholic Emancipation Act of 1829, it wasn't long before the faith was again established in Leeds, helped along by waves of immigration from countries including Ireland and France.

The first Catholic place of worship built in Leeds after the Reformation was Lady Lane Chapel, founded in 1790, followed by St Mary's Chapel, founded in 1794 by Father Bernard Albert Underhill, with the financial help of local mill owner Joseph Holdforth.

Between 1750 and 1850, the number of Catholics in England

increased four-fold, leading to a large increase in the number of churches and the creation of thirteen new dioceses in 1850 – with Leeds in the Diocese of Beverley, until this diocese was split in 1878, creating the Diocese of Leeds and the Diocese of Middlesbrough. There were more than 98,000 Catholics in the Leeds Diocese when it was created, with seventy-four churches. Just a century later, numbers had increased to 266,000 worshippers and over 250 places of worship.

Leeds L&FHL has copies of the *Catholic Post* newspaper and the *Catholic Voice*, which are distributed to parishes across the region and contain items on parish life, church appointments and events such as anniversaries, outings and the opening and closure of churches.

Roman Catholic records

The city's main resource for Roman Catholic records for Leeds and its suburbs is the Diocese of Leeds Archives. As just noted, the Leeds Diocese was created in 1878 and nowadays covers a huge area including parts of North and West Yorkshire, the East Riding of Yorkshire, Greater Manchester and Lancashire.

The archives predate the creation of the Diocese of Leeds and include the holdings of the former Diocese of Beverley (established 1850) and the earlier Northern and Yorkshire District (founded in 1688). Among the most useful resources are parish registers of births, marriages and deaths, as well as details of individual priests, many of whom came from other Yorkshire towns and cities including Bradford and Selby. The archives has a small reference library which has out-of-print and difficult to find works on the history of Roman Catholicism in the area, and histories of local churches. There are several theses and dissertations to consult, several of which focus on Irish Catholics who settled in Leeds.

The heart of the archive comprises Bishops' Papers dating from 1780 through to the 1960s, all of which are indexed and calendared. These documents comprise correspondence and printed documents dealing mainly with the administration of the diocese during the nineteenth century, and where these are indexed, it is possible to trace specific individuals. The diocesan records can be a rich source

Religion

Hinsley Hall, the home of the Diocese of Leeds Archives.

of information on population history and the history of an individual parish.

It is possible to trace the history of a Roman Catholic parish or school in the diocese through archive holdings which include school records (including log books and admission registers), parish magazines and souvenir brochures – which often name individual parishioners, and plans, drawings and photographs relating to individual churches. A particular highlight is a century's worth of records for St Michael's College in Leeds from 1905 through to 2005.

The collection is particularly strong on the history of the Leeds

Roman Catholic cathedral, St Anne's, which was built between 1900 and 1904. The microfilm records held at the Diocese of Leeds Archives include records for Killingbeck Cemetery, as well as St Anne's Cathedral, Mount St Mary, St Patrick and Holy Family. Mount St Mary Church was known as the 'famine church' as it was built in the Richmond Hill area of Leeds in the 1850s, at a time of Irish immigration following the potato famine.

Leeds Diocesan Archives, Hinsley Hall, 62 Headingley Lane, Leeds LS6 2BX; tel.: 0113 261 8031; email: robert.finnigan@dioceseofleeds.org.uk; website: www.dioceseofleeds.org.uk/archives

WYAS Leeds holds a number of important Roman Catholic records for more recent years, including records for Catholic schools in Leeds including St Mary's Richmond Hill and St Richard's at Holbeck and closed marriage registers for Catholic churches at Richmond Hill, Seacroft and Kirkstall from the early 1970s to early 1990s.

Microfilm copies of Roman Catholic marriage registers for Leeds are held by Leeds WYAS and comprise: St Anne's Cathedral (RC11) 1834–1907 baptisms and 1814–1907 marriages; Mount St Mary (RC12) 1851–1907 baptisms and 1854–1903 marriages and 1869–99 deaths; and St Patrick's (RC13) 1873–99 births and 1831–1906 deaths. A guide to the Roman Catholic WYAS collections can be found at: http://bit.ly/myleedsrcrecords.

Methodism

In the early eighteenth century, the presence of non-conformism in the town was restricted to travelling preachers, many of whom found themselves unwelcome guests.

Writing in his journal in February 1746, Methodism founder John Wesley said:

> Sat 22 Feb 1746 to Leeds. I preached at five. As we went home a great mob followed and threw whatever came to hand. I was struck several times, once or twice in the face, but not hurt at all.

However, three years later, his reception had improved and he was writing of 'a crowded audience of high and low, rich and poor'.

Religion

John Wesley, the founder of Methodism.

A Leeds circuit was established and a permanent meeting place established at Ingram's Hall at Hunslet. Despite the permanence of this arrangement, Methodist worshippers were still subject to regular harassment on their way to and from the chapel.

Methodist records

WYAS Leeds has what are believed to be some of the oldest Methodist records in the world. All of the Leeds circuits have deposits here, including minute books, day school records, preaching licences and accounts. A Methodist chapel was created at St Peters Square in 1771, followed by a Baptist chapel at St Peters Square in 1779. By the middle of the nineteenth century, Methodism had divided into a bewildering range of denominations, including Wesleyan Methodists, Wesleyan Reformers and Primitive Methodists, each with their own places of worship. The Hanover Place Chapel on Park Lane, built in 1847 at a time of large-scale immigration to Leeds, had seating for 1,000 worshippers.

Methodist registers begin in the late eighteenth century but can be difficult to work with, as the system of circuits where preachers visited different towns and villages in an area changed frequently. It is necessary to know in which circuit your ancestor would have lived and this is an area where the knowledge of local record office staff can be invaluable.

Records Relating to Other Non-Conformism

By the time Queen Victoria came to the throne, Leeds was, according to historians Steven Bart and Kevin Brady, 'a noted centre of nonconformity' with the Church of England having only eight of the town's thirty-five places of worship.

Baptists

In 1780, work began on a stone chapel and the Ebenezer Baptist Chapel opened in 1782 on Ebenezer Street, east of Vicar Lane, one of the first streets of back-to-back housing in the town. This was the first permanent Baptist place of worship in Leeds and more were soon to follow. The oldest Baptist record held by WYAS Leeds is the 1740–1795 Church Book which relates to Gildersome (WYL1213/2/1). From this date onwards, records for the city include registers of church members, account books, Sunday school records, deacons' minute books and church meeting records, with the nineteenth century particularly well represented. Other non-conformist records held at WYAS Leeds relate to the Moravians, Presbyterians,

Religion

Unitarians, United Reformed Church, Independent and Congregational.

One of the main archives relating to non-conformism is the Quaker Collection in the Special Collections department at Leeds University library. This is one of the largest Quaker record repositories outside London and comprises two main sections: the Carlton Hill & Clifford Street Collections; and photocopied and microfilmed sets of Quaker birth, marriage and death certificates. The Carlton Hill & Clifford Street records are original documentary archives relating to parts of West and North Yorkshire, as well as York and Thirsk. When searching for an individual or family within these lists, remember that, because the catchment areas for meetings could be very wide, an individual may not have attended a meeting in the district where they lived.

Where an ancestor is listed, though, there is often the added bonus of finding other family members listed alongside. The details given usually include the person's name, the names of their parents, their occupation, address and (if applicable) why they left their previous meeting area.

Another useful resource is the Quaker Heritage Project (http://www.hull.ac.uk/oldlib/archives/quaker), an evolving online source of information about the location of Quaker archives and records in Yorkshire and archives outside the country which are of Yorkshire interest.

The website allows you to search by town or village, the name of an individual, the name of a Quaker meeting or a particular archive repository. At the time of writing, there are seventy-six Leeds collections listed, dating from the 1650s through to the 1980s. These include records for individual schools and fellowship houses, family papers and registers of births, marriages and burials.

Non-Christian Religions

Records for non-Christian faiths, such as Islam or Judaism, can be particularly challenging to research as many of these are written in languages other than English. Some of these religious archives are still kept by the relevant place of worship but it is usually possible to

Non-Christian records can be a challenge due to language difficulties.

make an appointment to view these, and help may be available with any difficulties encountered due to language.

Islam

Although present-day Leeds has a population of around 30,000 Muslims, this community has grown only in recent years, meaning that family history sources other than the standard birth, marriage and death records are few. The city's first mosque was built in 1958 at Leopold Street and moved to larger premises in 1974 at Spencer Place.

Religion

The Leeds Islamic Centre, based at the central Jamia Mosque, is a good starting point for finding where religious records are kept. *Leeds Islamic Centre, 46–48 Spencer Place, Leeds LS7 4BR; tel.: 0113 262 3100; website: www.leedsic.com*

Judaism

Now one of the largest Jewish communities outside London and Manchester, the Jewish community in Leeds grew from small beginnings into an influential social group, with strong commercial links to key city businesses, particularly tailoring.

The first Jewish services in Leeds were held in private homes, with meetings eventually established in a small loft in Bridge Street.

Until 1840, Jews had to be taken to Hull to be buried as there was no provision for Jewish burials in Leeds and surrounds. At the time of the 1841 census, there were less than ten Jewish families in Leeds but as the city began to expand during the Victorian age, Jewish families were attracted to the area and the employment opportunities offered by the blossoming textile trade. The first Jewish marriage in Leeds took place in 1842.

The majority of Jews who came to Leeds were escaping the pogroms of Eastern Europe which began with the assassination of the Russian Tsar Alexander II in 1881. They fled Europe, from countries including Russia, Lithuania and Poland, moving to the port of Rotterdam and on to Hull, ultimately seeking the chance to begin a new life in the USA. However, many never made it that far. When they travelled across England to Liverpool, with its access to the Atlantic, they found plentiful work opportunities on offer in Leeds, which would have seemed particularly attractive to newcomers of the Jewish faith as more and more of their kin were already settled here.

These incomers headed for the Leylands, where a Jewish community had begun to establish itself. The city's first official synagogue opened in Back Rockingham Street in 1846, with a bigger place of worship built in Belgrave Street in 1860. The Leylands, close to the city centre, was an area noted for poverty and overcrowding. Like the Irish immigrants, Jews often suffered from terrible living conditions and poor pay, if indeed they could find work. The

Leylands was home for hundreds of Jews but when, in the early 1900s, Hope Street was demolished, the community began to move towards the Meanwood Valley and from there onwards to Moortown and Alwoodley. Nowadays there are around 7,000 Jews to be found in Leeds, mainly settled in the affluent suburbs of Moortown and Alwoodley.

Locating Jewish family history records
WYAS Leeds has a large number of records relating to Judaism in Leeds, including reports for various Jewish councils and societies which helped administer life in Leeds, including the Leeds Jewish Education Board, the Leeds Jewish Hospital Board, the Leeds Jewish Refugees Committee and the Leeds Jewish Kosher Kitchen.

There are also certificates of naturalisation (WYL2065), films of Jewish life in Leeds (WYL2039) and records relating to tailors Montague Burton for the years 1896 to 1983 (WYL1951).

For lists of individual synagogues which may hold marriage records, visit the Jewish Gen website (www.jewishgen.org/jcr-uk/leeds.htm), which has a comprehensive list of individual congregations, as well as details of various cemeteries which have Jewish burials. Jewish Gen also has plenty of information on the history of Jews in Leeds and the various resources you can explore.

Jewish births are listed in the civil registers from 1837. However, prior to this, few communities kept records and these only from 1764 onwards. A search for marriage and burial records is likely to prove more fruitful. Because Jews (and Quakers) were exempt from the Hardwicke Act of 1753, Jewish congregations were able to keep their own marriage records, and until civil registration these were kept in duplicate by the bride and sometimes by the synagogue. Many marriages were carried out in private homes and outside of officialdom and, for these, no records exist.

There are two magazines which can be accessed for information on the lives of Jews, *The Gentleman's Magazine* (held by the Yorkshire Archaeological Society in Leeds) and the *Jewish Chronicle*. You can carry out a trial search of the latter at http://bit.ly/myleedsjewish.

Religion

Jewish Genealogical Society of Great Britain
The UK's only national Jewish genealogical society, the Jewish Genealogical Society of Great Britain (JGSGB) has been established for over twenty years and brings researchers together through meetings, a newsletter, journal, library and website (www.jgsgb.org.uk).

The Leeds branch of the group meets in the city for talks and visits relating to the history of Jewish people in the Yorkshire area and particularly in Leeds. This group doesn't hold any physical records, but instead refers members to the website and library in London.

At a national level, the JGSGB offers members the use of a Jewish genealogical database, an online discussion group and a library (in central London) of over 1,000 books which is classed as one of the finest Jewish genealogy resources in Europe. The society also publishes its own genealogy guides.

As well as books, there are Jewish genealogy magazines, memorial books (records of lost communities in Eastern Europe) and family histories and trees prepared by individuals across the continent. Anyone with Jewish kin is invited to submit a tree to the society. In the existing family trees, where any surname is featured three or more times in a tree, it is indexed alphabetically. Many of these trees can be viewed in paper form at the library; others are available in electronic form on the library's computers. Some are illustrated and annotated and where the tree's creator is willing to be contacted by a researcher, contact details can be obtained. You can see an alphabetical list of over 3,000 surnames on the website in the 'library' section of the resources tab.

Membership of the JGSGB is £35 per year or £40 for annual family membership. Researchers can join the society, and then ask to be put in touch with the Leeds branch.

The Leeds Database
A useful online website (http://british-jewry.org.uk/leedsjewry/index.php) began as a series of Jewish family trees relating to the Leeds area and has expanded to include photos, cemetery records and

discussions. You begin by entering a first name and surname into the search box and can then browse the various categories. As with all online records, double checking any information before adding to your own records is essential, but this is a useful site for helping to track ancestors between birth, marriage, burial and censuses.

Chapter 8

LEISURE TIME

No matter what their age or occupation, our ancestors would have looked for ways to spend their leisure time, whether travelling into the town centre to enjoy concerts or films, or taking part in or watching sports. This chapter explores some of the main leisure pursuits of the past few centuries and offers some ideas for finding out more about leisure time in Leeds.

Sport
Although informal team games have taken place in our town and cities for centuries, it is only within the last 150 years that organised sport has been a leisure pursuit – for both players and spectators. The three most popular team games have been rugby, cricket and football, with both professional and amateur teams existing in the city.

Local newspapers are a rich source of information on both amateur and professional sports fixtures. These often also carry news snippets about particular players who had broken a sporting record, reached a special anniversary or won a sports prize. Leeds L&FHL has dozens of sports history books relating to the city, whilst WYAS Leeds is home to collections of sporting memorabilia, including fixtures and results information, membership records for both professional and amateur sports clubs, scrapbooks, press cuttings and photographs. Do also consider exploring the records of the school, workplace or church that an ancestor attended, as many such organisations had their own sports clubs.

Dozens of sports clubs have chosen to deposit their historic records with WYAS for safekeeping and most of these are on open access. Among the highlights of the WYAS sports collections are the Sports in Times Past Collection (WYC1403) which is a collection of

The WYAS collections range from cockfighting to cricket.

oral history interviews along with photos; the Spencer Stanhope estate archive (spst/12) which includes information on older sports including cockfighting and horse racing; and the Wilfred Towriss scrapbooks (WYB13) which cover the years 1937 to 1946 and include football, cricket and boxing memorabilia.

The Leodis website (www.leodis.net) has dozens of sports photographs, ranging from aerial views of sports grounds to team photos. Yorkshire Film Archive is a rich source of online photographic and video history, with over 100 films, including amateur boxing, 1970s professional football and rugby footage, archery, cycling and horse racing.

Leisure Time

Cricket
Test Cricket has been played at Headingley, now the home of Yorkshire County Cricket Club, since 1899. The county team has a proud tradition, having produced more England players and won more trophies than any other county. The cricket heritage of the city is well represented at the new Yorkshire County Cricket Museum which is located in the east stand of Headingley Cricket Ground, familiar to generations of sports fans – and also on the same plot of land as the city's main rugby stadium.
Yorkshire County Cricket Museum, Headingley Cricket Ground, Headingley, Leeds LS6 3DP; tel.: 0113 504 3099; website: www.yorkshireccc.com

Football
Despite that fact that Leeds now has famous rugby and football clubs, in the Victorian era, rugby was the dominant sport, with football very much an amateur concern.

Long before the foundation of Leeds United Football Club and its predecessors, a 'Leeds Football Club' was in existence, as a letter to the *Leeds Mercury* on 20 May 1864 demonstrates:

> At present the club numbers 250 members, of all ages from thirteen to fifty, and of every class … anyone is allowed to join the club who will play without roughness and as the subscription is only 1s, every barrier against the prominence of classes is removed.

Newspaper articles (which can be accessed on the Nineteenth-Century British Newspapers website, see Chapter 9) give information on meetings, matches and changes to the membership over the years.

The first football match played in Leeds in front of spectators is believed to have been an exhibition match on Boxing Day 1877, which saw Leeds players face a Sheffield team.

Another football club simply named 'Leeds' was formed in Kirkstall in 1885, by Leonard Cooper, who persuaded talented players from other clubs to join, including SV Smith (of Notts

County), RW Burrows (Old Foresters) and E Cautley (Old Carthusians). The first match scheduled for 3 October 1885 was cancelled after the other team, from Hull, failed to turn up. However the club soon settled into a schedule of regular matches with other neighbouring towns and played at Kirkstall Cricket Ground before folding after two years.

This, of course, wasn't the end of the story. The club Leeds Albion was formed at the works of the firm Armley Wilson & Mathiesons, with its first game taking place in October 1888. The first derby was Leeds versus Albion on 10 November 1888, with Leeds winning 3-1. The following year Leeds Steelworks team was founded in Hunslet, created largely from men of that industry.

When the West Yorkshire league was formed in 1894, teams from Leeds, Hunslet, Rothwell and Pontefract began to play the game competitively. Leeds folded in 1898 and so it would actually be Hunslet who would be the forerunners of Leeds City, who entered the football league in 1905. Although Hunslet itself folded in 1902, many of its members got together to form Leeds City, taking over the former grounds of Holbeck Rugby Club at Elland Road, home of the present Leeds United. The team joined the football league on 29 May 1905 and began work on improvements to the ground.

Leeds United Football Club was founded in 1919, in the wake of the First World War, after the demise of its predecessor, the Leeds City Football Club. The club joined the football league on 31 May 1920, joining the second division and four years, later the first division.

Parks

Despite its reputation as a busy and crowded place, Leeds has, since the Victorian era, prided itself on its parks and public gardens. Particularly in the areas of the city where back to back housing dominated, a park was often the only place where our ancestors could enjoy some greenery and fresh air.

The city's two principal parks are Rounday Park and Golden Acre Park. Rounday Park was purchased by the city council in 1871 and was opened to the public the following year, offering over 700 acres

Leisure Time

Rounday Park at the turn of the twentieth century. © Tuck DB Postcards

of grounds which had previously been a country estate since the time of William the Conqueror. With opportunities for boating, enjoying tropical plants, walks and music concerts, the park has been a favourite for generations. It was connected to the city centre by a tramline in 1891 and in 1926 some 130,000 people enjoyed a military tattoo held there, starting a tradition of musical entertainment which has continued in the decades since.

Over fifty years after the opening of Roundhay Park, a privately owned amusement park opened at Golden Acre near Bramhope. The park boasted a miniature railway, boats and a swimming pool but was closed down during the Second World War, reopening under council care in 1945.

WYAS Leeds has archive material relating to these two parks, and other city parks, including plans, maps, deeds, photographs, minute books, souvenir memorabilia and press cuttings.

Theatre and Cinema

For our ancestors, an evening at the cinema or theatre was an escape from the realities of bringing up a family and earning a living. From the late 1700s, when theatres in Leeds were established following the popularity of travelling theatre, through to the golden age of cinema in the 1930s and 1940s, when there were dozens of cinemas across the city, the world of entertainment can tell us much about what amused our ancestors and the type of shows they might have enjoyed.

The first theatre in Leeds opened in 1771 on Hunslet Lane. Before this, the townspeople would have had access to plays performed by travelling troupes. Although this theatre was popular, it would be over twenty years before another establishment opened – the Albion Street Music Hall, founded in 1792. The Victorian era, with its huge population growth, would see the opening of several music halls and theatres including Thorntons New Music Hall (later the City Varieties) in 1865, the Theatre Royal (1876) and the Coliseum which was opened by the Prince and Princess of Wales in 1885. Holbeck's Queen's Theatre (founded in 1898) appealed to those who didn't wish to travel into the city in the evening.

Leisure Time

The Grand Theatre opened after serious fires at two other theatres nearby. © M Taylor

Leeds Grand Theatre opened on 18 November 1878, offering both seated and standing room for audiences. The seeds for this building had been sown twenty years earlier when Queen Victoria opened the Town Hall and her spouse Prince Albert was heard to remark that 'Leeds seemed in need of a good theatre'. The opening attracted the attention of newspapers in cities as distant as Hull and Leeds. The *Hull Packet & East Riding Times* reported on 22 November 1878:

> From the front row of the orchestra stalls to the back of the gallery there is not a seat from which a good view of the stage cannot be obtained. The pit is very commodious and comfortable and the architects seem to have recognised the fact that from the pit the manager must look for a large amount of the support given to him.

London paper *The Era* carried this report on 24 November: 'The people of Leeds are to be congratulated on having in their midst one of the noblest theatrical buildings in this or any other country.'

The opening came after two disastrous fires had gutted Leeds theatres – the Theatre Royal in Hunslet Lane had burned down in May 1875, followed by Joseph Hobson's Ampitheatre on the corner of Lands Lane shortly afterwards. In May 1876 a company was formed to acquire land and build a theatre. The Grand took thirteen months to build, at a cost of £60,000, and was created by George Corson and James Robertson Watson in a Victorian Gothic style. The theatre must have been full of atmosphere; as well as traditional seating there were pit stalls – wooden benches where members of the public of limited means, but who wanted a great night out, were squeezed on. This sort of evening wasn't for the faint-hearted – a 'packer in' man was employed to fill the benches as full as possible, even resorting to pushing if necessary, in order to fill the benches to capacity.

The first pantomime performed at The Grand was *Blue Beard*, followed by *Dick Whittington* the following Christmas. These well-loved pantomimes carried on even through the war years, with old favourites, usually on a fairy tale theme, repeated again and again.

One of the city's Victorian theatres which can still be enjoyed today is Leeds City Varieties. Founded in 1865, the Varieties is a music hall theatre which was originally built as an adjunct to the Swan Inn. The interior of the grade II listed building is much as it was in its

Victorian heyday, and over the years it has played host to the likes of Charlie Chaplin, Harry Houdini, Lilly Langtry and Harry Lauder.

Theatre archive material
For a good starting point to theatre history in Leeds, visit the Leodis website (www.leodis.net/discovery) where you will find a 'Leeds theatres' section, which includes images and prints as well as an extensive bibliography and image list. You can also read about the history of individual theatres including the Albion Street Music Hall, Coliseum and Empire Palace. The same website also hosts the Leeds playbills collection (www.leodis.net/playbills) which is covered below.

WYAS Leeds has a wide range of theatre memorabilia for Leeds City Varieties and the city's other theatres, including photos of music hall artists, programmes, books of press cuttings, accounts and photographs of theatre interiors.

At Leeds L&FHL you can find copies of local newspapers which include the *Leeds Mercury* and *Yorkshire Post*, which are on microfilm. You can search these for details of specific performances, theatres or performers. Another source of information is trade directories, which list local theatres, along with the name of each owner. Because trade directories, unlike censuses, were usually issued annually, it is possible to track a theatre through the years and build up a picture of how the streets around the theatre changed, as businesses came and went.

The library also has a good collection of theatre programmes from theatres including Leeds Civic Theatre, the Leeds Empire, the Grand, and West Yorkshire Playhouse. Souvenir brochures for these establishments also commemorate theatre milestones, such as the opening of the Scala Theatre in 1922 and the Leeds Playhouse in 1970. Also available is a collection of newsletters and newsletter cuttings for you to explore if you have an idea of the years in which you are interested.

One of the library's rarest collections, and one which needs staff supervision to view, is the Leslie Popplewell Autograph Collection (SRQ091.5P819). The collection comprises six boxes, largely devoted to autographs of stars to whom Leslie had sent a birthday card and 'birthday book' for them to sign. One of the boxes contains letters and photos from theatre stars who had replied to Leslie.

The autographs cover the years from 1940 to the 1970s and include stage actors, singers, entertainers and film and TV stars, such as Mae West, Dudley Moore, Margaret Lockwood and Donald Pleasance. Three large scrapbooks in the collection are devoted to publicity and newspaper articles relating to stage productions, largely in London. Perhaps more pertinently for Leeds theatre, considering the city's classical music background, the autographs of classical musicians and conductors are also included. The material isn't indexed but, for anyone interested in theatre, this is a unique piece of history.

Leeds Playbills
Leeds Playbills is a website which forms part of the Leodis digitisation project and is making available playbills from a range of the city's theatres including The Grand, City Varieties, the Theatre Royal and the Princess – from the 1780s through to the 1990s. Whether you want to trace the theatre company that an ancestor worked for, or to discover what type of shows were staged at a particular time, this is a helpful site for initial research.

You can search by theatre name or the name of an actor/actress, and narrow down the search to particular dates, or simply browse through all theatres in the city. There are also circus bills for travelling shows and music hall bills which include 'Hamilton's Continental Excursions' of 1868, where the audience was 'transported' to London, moving through to Switzerland, Italy and Germany, with actors including Professor Heyl and Alfred Hamilton; and an evening of spectral drama in 1866 which boasted of 'living heads floating in the air' and an illusion intriguingly named 'we are here but not here!'

You can see the originals of the playbills at Leeds Local Studies Library and order copies of the playbills through the website: http://www.leodis.net/playbills.

Live Music
For hundreds of years, the folk of Leeds have appreciated live music

performances, including choral performances at the Town Hall, open-air brass band concerts in the city's parks or more recent pop concerts.

Leeds L&FHL is home to a series of bound volumes of past programmes for the Leeds Music Festival, an eagerly anticipated event held at the Town Hall which had its roots in the opening of that building in 1858, when a concert raised £2,000 for Leeds medical charities, with a headline performance of 'The May Queen' by Sterndale Bennett.

The festival's reputation grew over the years and went from attracting chorus members from the city itself to a wider net, with singers being trained ahead of the concerts in Huddersfield, Halifax and Bradford and then travelling in for performances.

Tickets for the concerts were on sale in Great George Street before the performances, and clients could also buy books featuring the words and music to the performances they'd be enjoying.

The programmes are full of colourful details, not only of which performers took part – there are lists ranging from headline acts to individual chorus members – but also more practical matters. For example, the 1898 programme advises:

> In view of the inconvenience that would be caused by ladies wearing tall hats, an appeal is made for them to adopt, for the morning concerts, some small head gear.

The programmes also include alphabetical lists of guarantors and details of how much they pledged. The popularity of the events can be seen through the extensive travel arrangements listed, showing which trains were available for those travelling home to Bradford, Sheffield, Ilkley or further into the Yorkshire Dales.

Cinema

Leeds is home to two of the country's oldest continuously operating cinemas – the Cottage Cinema, Headingley, which dates to 1912 and the Hyde Park Picture House, which opened in 1914. These two picture houses are what remain of the dozens of cinemas which dotted Leeds, serving both the suburbs and the city centre. From huge picture houses such as the Savoy on Boar Lane and the Majestic on City Square (recently gutted by fire), to smaller concerns such as the Picture House at Holbeck and the Star Cinema on York Road, picture houses enjoyed huge popularity in the years before the widespread introduction of TV, in the 1950s, changed our viewing habits.

The city's oldest cinema, which no longer fulfils its original use, was The Plaza on New Briggate, which opened to the public on 15 April 1907, offering 'new century talking and singing pictures' with a debut performance of the film *Little Tich*, featuring music hall star Harry Relph. The building, which had originally been a Victorian concert hall, survived as a cinema until 1985 and is now part of the Assembly Rooms performance space, home to Opera North.

The year 1913 was a boom time for cinema in Leeds, with new cinemas opening at Abbey Road (Abbey Picture House), Boar Lane (City Cinema), Kirkstall Road (Imperial), Sheepscar (Newtown Picture Palace) and dozens more followed in the years to come.

The height of the cinema boom was the 1920s and 1930s, when cinemas were built to be as attractive and ornate as possible, offering the ordinary working man and woman a taste of Hollywood glamour. With programmes usually changing at least twice a week, a trip to the cinema was an eagerly anticipated and affordable treat for many. Children had their own Saturday matinee, which was usually a kids-only affair, with any pocket money going on sweets and drinks for the performance.

The Odeon, on The Headrow, opened in 1932 as the Paramount, at the height of the golden age of cinema. With seating for 2,500 and a grand Wurlitzer Organ, it welcomed over one million cinema goers in its first year of operation, beginning with a showing of *The Smiling Lieutenant* with Maurice Chevalier. In 1940, the cinema was renamed for its owners Odeon Theatres and, in the 1960s, hosted two huge concerts featuring The Beatles and Roy Orbison.

One of the city's grandest cinemas was The Majestic, which still stands on City Square, although its days as a cinema ended in 1969. The Majestic was designed by architects Pascal J. Stienlet and JC Maxwell and opened on 5 June 1922. Its grand interior included a

Leisure Time

GENERAL POST OFFICE AND THE MAJESTIC CINEMA, CITY SQUARE, LEEDS

The historic Majestic (left) was recently gutted by fire.

huge auditorium which could seat over 2,300 patrons, a grand plaster frieze and space for a symphony orchestra. Sadly, the cinema was damaged by a fire in September 2014 and at the time of writing, its future is uncertain.

Local newspapers (available at WYAS Leeds and Leeds L&FHL) are a rich source of information on the opening (and closure) of the city's different cinemas. You can also look at cinema advertisements showing the variety of films on offer over the years. The 1950s is a particularly interesting decade to research, as cinema managers in their attempts to compete with the competition of television, often invited celebrities to the opening of films.

In the early 1960s, film star Patricia Medina paid a visit to John

Collier's Tailors at Cardigan Fields, Kirkstall, as part of a promotional film tour. Her photo, where she is pictured with a number of Collier's employees, can be seen on the Leodis website (LEO7292).

WYAS Leeds holds a small number of papers relating to the building and running of Leeds cinemas, including an agreement to build a cinema at Montreal Avenue in 1933 (LLD1/1/A9338) and a 1946 agreement for Belle Isle cinema (LLD1/1/A15261).

Chapter 9

LEEDS ONLINE

Over the last few years, the number and quality of Leeds-related family history websites has grown greatly. Whether you'd like to see photos of the street where your ancestor lived, track down a 'lost' ancestor who you have been unable to locate through traditional means or carry out some background research to bring your findings to life, there are plenty of ideas here.

Internet research is fascinating and can be very inspiring, as well as giving you new ideas for taking your research further. Do, though, make sure that any information you find online and plan to use in your family tree is backed up by checking the original sources where possible, so that you avoid researching the wrong ancestors.

Ancestry
www.ancestry.co.uk/yorkshire: Ancestry have recently digitised more than eight million West Yorkshire parish records, going beyond the traditional birth, marriage and death registers, with confirmation, burial and baptism records, some dating back as far as the Civil War. Some of this information is surprisingly detailed. For example, documents in the Dade Registers include names, addresses and occupations of parents, and even grandparents of those mentioned.

The West Yorkshire history section (http://bit.ly/myleedstimeline) is a useful timeline of major Yorkshire events from the earliest days of the textile trade through to the multicultural cities of the new millennium. Among the topics of interest to those with Leeds ancestors are the Civil War Battle of Leeds (1643), an outbreak of bubonic plague in the city in 1645 and the creation of the Iron Horse at Middleton Railway in 1758.

Ancestry can be accessed free of charge in any Leeds Library – just ask library staff for details.

Arthur Lloyd covers over a century of entertainment history.

Arthur Lloyd

www.arthurlloyd.co.uk: A music hall and theatre history website which holds information and photos relating to the history of these two forms of entertainment, with data for much of the UK. The Leeds section lists fourteen theatres, six of which are still in use. Each individual theatre has its own page with details of when it was founded, which stars appeared there, as well as old photos and, in some cases, other memorabilia such as press cuttings and programmes or playbills.

Cyndi's List

www.cyndislist.com: This is one of the world's biggest online resources for genealogy links and a well-regarded site which has been established for almost twenty years. You can access the information either via geographical area or through a keyword search. With over 600 links for Yorkshire, the information can seem quite overwhelming but is organised logically, with listings including military, obituaries, religion, schools, taxes and wills.

Discovering Leeds

www.leodis.net/discovery/default.asp: A great starting point for beginning your online research into life in bygone Leeds, Discovering Leeds is part of the Leodis Project from Leeds Library & Information Service. The site covers over 1,000 years of Leeds history through nine subject areas: Briggate, Leeds Town Hall, The Headrow, The Waterfront, Leeds Theatres, Poverty & Riches, Leeds Classical Music, The Markets, and Industrial Leeds. Each of these sections has an accessible overview of the topic, alongside historic prints and photographs relating to the subject and suggestions for further reading and study.

The Poverty & Riches section is particularly helpful for family history researchers, documenting living and working conditions in Leeds from the seventeenth century through to the early 1900s and

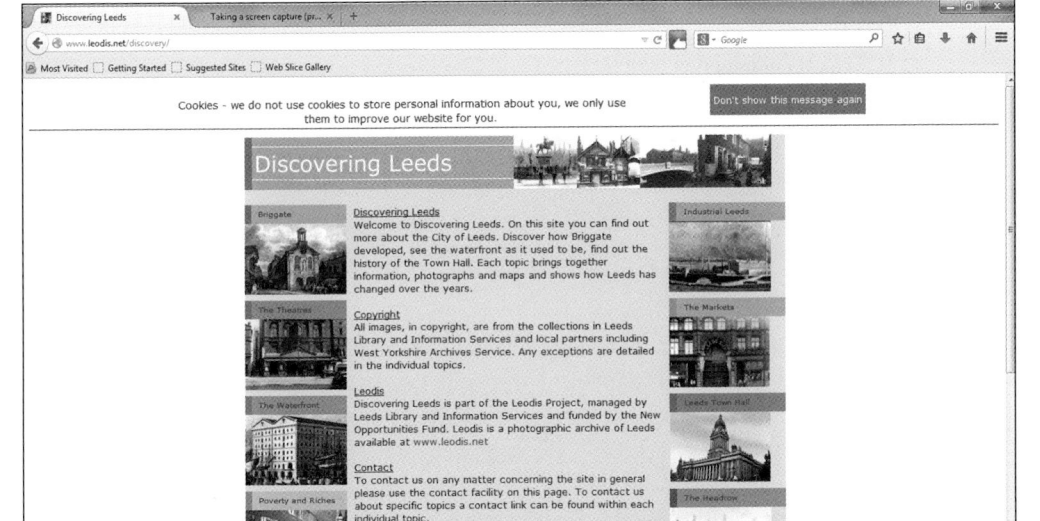

Discover more about the city through nine different topics.

attempting to discover why poverty was so rife in the city and what was done to attempt to alleviate it. From the first workhouses of the 1600s, built at the same time that wealthy merchants were beginning to create fine houses in the city, to the huge social and health problems created by the growth of industry, we learn about the flight of the middle classes to the suburbs, the creation of crowded back to back terraces for an influx of workers, and the eventual slum clearances of the early twentieth century.

Family Search
www.familysearch.org: The 1881 census for the UK is available free of charge via Family Search, which also provides free access to the International Genealogical Index – an incomplete but huge database of baptism and marriage records prior to 1850.

Find My Past
www.findmypast.com: A pay per view website which goes beyond the usual birth, marriage and death records (although these are covered for 1837 to 2006) and includes census records (1841 to 1911), trade directories and electoral rolls. You can buy vouchers to use on this site at the Leeds L&FH Library.

At the time of writing there are nine sections of records: birth, marriage, death & parish records; census, land & surveys; churches & religion; directories & social history; education & work; institutions & organisations; military, armed forces & conflict; travel & migration; and newspapers & periodicals. In each of these categories you have the option to enter an ancestor's name, date of birth (or estimate), optional keywords and optional record names.

Francis Frith Collection
www.francisfrith.com: Although this is primarily a website which focuses on selling old photographs and books, it has hundreds of old photos of Leeds which can be viewed at a large size and which are difficult to find elsewhere. Both the city and the suburbs are well represented, with almost 600 photos and memories to explore. You can search by the keyword 'Leeds', try street or building names or the names of the city's districts. Many of the photographs also

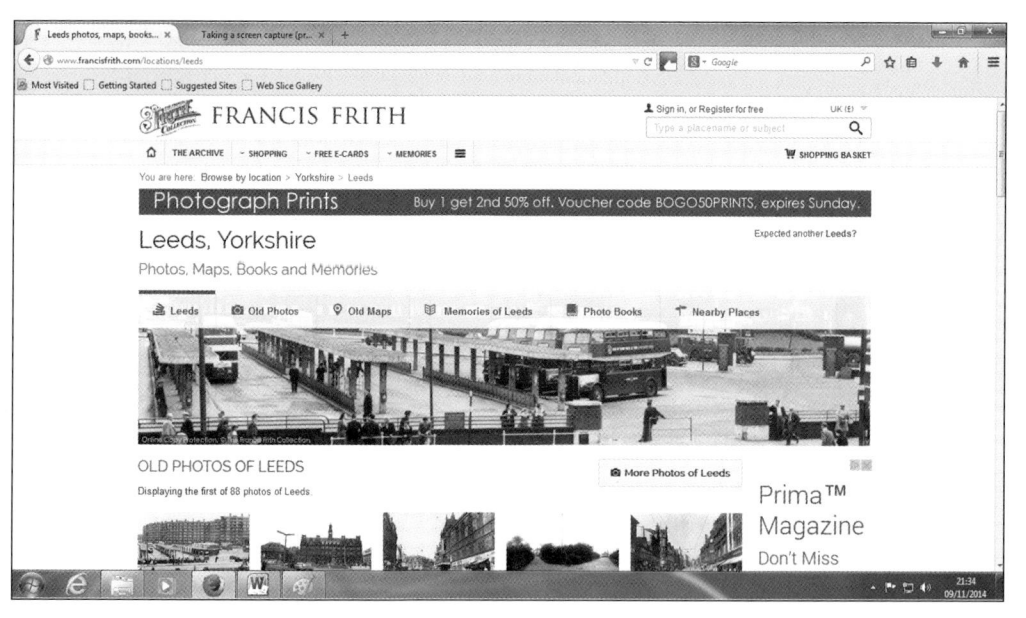

The website is a treasure trove of historic photos.

include informative comments submitted by members of the public, with memories of the site pictured or historical information to supplement the captions.

Examples of the memories include 'Christmas in Second World War Leeds', 'Growing up in 1950s Gildersome' and 'Cookridge School in the 1940s'.

Free BMD

www.freebmd.org.uk: A free database of births, marriages and deaths for England from 1837 onwards. Although coverage is not yet complete, volunteers are actively completing transcriptions and so it is worth coming back to this site periodically. If you do find the ancestor you're looking for, the site provides a national certificate reference number for the birth, marriage or death in question, allowing you to send for a copy of the certificate.

Free UK Census Online Project

www.freecen.org.uk: A free database covering the UK censuses for 1841, 1851, 1861, 1871 and 1891. Although coverage is not complete, this can provide a useful starting point for following the fortunes of ancestors without paying for census information. As volunteers are working on transcriptions on an ongoing basis, it is worth checking this site periodically in case new relevant records have been added.

Genuki Leeds pages

www.genuki.org.uk/big/eng/YKS/WRY/Leeds: Genuki is a virtual reference library of information for genealogists and, with its thousands of pages of information on England alone, the site can be an excellent starting point for further research.

At the time of writing, there are more than 40,000 pages of information in the Yorkshire section of the site, which begins with an overview of the county and its history, as well as information on how boundaries have changed over the centuries. The top level of the Yorkshire pages has broad categories on topics such as the census, religion, further reading and archives around the county.

In order to access Leeds material you'll need either to explore within these categories or perform a keyword search using the word 'Leeds' or another more defined topic of interest. There are over 2,000 results for a search with 'Leeds', including parish registers, census records, and transcriptions of war memorials. The further into the results lists you go, the less relevant the match – a star system indicates how relevant each link is before you click on it.

History Pin

www.historypin.com: An online 'global community' which invites users to post historic photographs of locations around the world and 'pin' them to a country map, so that other users can add their own photos and memories.

You can try a general search using the word 'Leeds' or narrow this down by date or subject. Both the city centre and the suburbs are fairly well represented, with dozens of photos and memories both of Leeds buildings, and events such as celebrations for the coronation of King George V, the Leeds tercentenary celebrations in

1926 and The Beatles concerts at the Leeds Odeon in 1965 and 1967. If you're interested in tracing the history of a house, you can also try a postcode or street name search; or help future researchers by pinning your own old photos.

History to Her Story
http://historytoherstory.hud.ac.uk: The story of the women of Yorkshire from the 1100s onwards, created in partnership with the University of Huddersfield and WYAS. Through digitised letters, diaries, documents and photographs, the website tells the story of both well-known and ordinary women through the centuries. There are more than 80,000 archive pages to explore and you can download a collections index to get you started. Among the Leeds holdings are records for the Workers Educational Association Leeds District, the records of the Leeds Babies Welcome Association, a commonplace book for Leeds suffragette Helen C Ford and an attendance book for Burley Lawn School.

Leeds Civic Trust
www.leedscivictrust.org.uk: The website of heritage group the Leeds Civic Trust has heritage news relating to the city's buildings and blue plaques; details of the group's city-wide heritage and history events, including guided walks; planning news and ongoing planning applications; and a bookshop which includes Leeds history and heritage titles that can be difficult to find elsewhere.

Leodis
www.leodis.net: Leodis is a photo archive of bygone Leeds which has, at the time of writing, almost 60,000 images of the city and its people. The project is delivered by Leeds Library & Information Service, who also offer the facility to buy the prints featured on the site.

There are various ways in which to use the site, ranging from a guided tour to get started, looking at the 'pick of the day' images or browsing through the different districts of the city. If you'd like to be more specific, you can use a search term such as a date or surname.

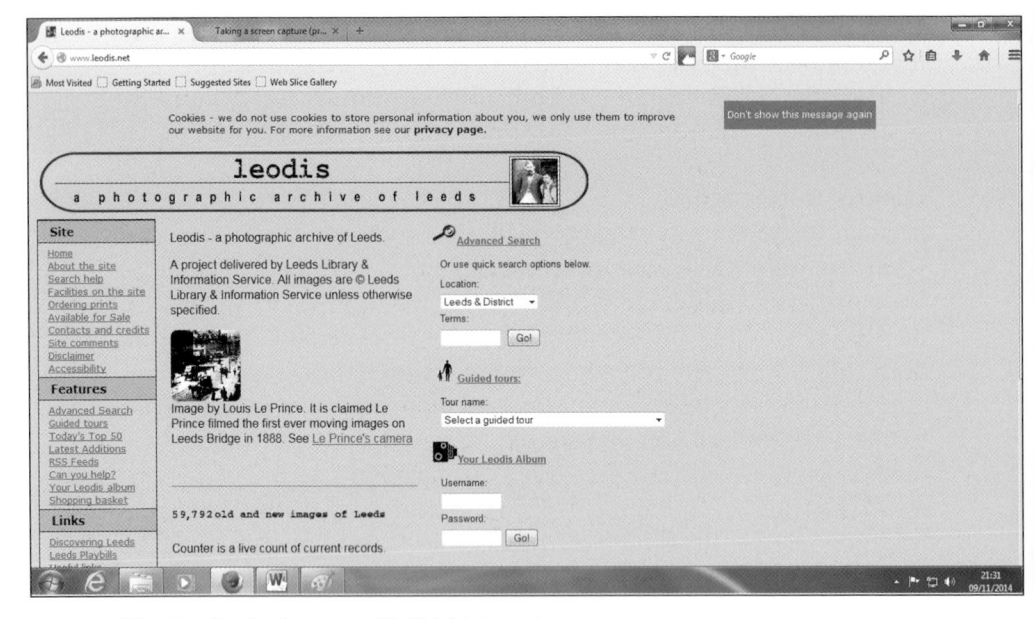

The Leodis site has over 60,000 historic images.

The 'city centre' option offers more than 2,000 images to view, including cinemas, street scenes, civic parades, the interiors and exteriors of shops, and advertising hoardings for various businesses. A photo of the Gipton Board School on the Harehills Road is typical of one of the street scene images – a large black and white image with details of when the school opened (1897) and where it was located (Harehills Road). There are also more than twenty comments from website users, giving further details and memories about the school.

The site links through to the Leeds Playbills site, a directory of theatre memorabilia (see Chapter 8) and Discovering Leeds, which is listed above.

Morley Community Archives

www.morleyarchives.org.uk: This is a great online resource run by a group of volunteers keen to preserve Morley's history and heritage. Although Morley is a town in its own right, it is within the Leeds

Metropolitan District and has strong links to the city. A large number of the photos were donated by local historian David Atkinson.

The online picture archive (http://bit.ly/myleedsmorleyarchives) is divided by decade (and in some cases, parts of a decade), beginning with pre-1900 images. You can browse each of the sections, which feature thumbnail versions of the images, then click onto an image for more information. Some of the details provided alongside the images have been taken from information gleaned at the reminiscence sessions which Morley Community Archives holds.

Among the images are public buildings, street scenes, individual properties, sports teams and paperwork such as a hymn sheet from Queen Victoria's Diamond Jubilee concert in Morley, and a bill sent to Joe Tetley for agricultural implements in 1884.

Now Then

http://nowthen.org: This is a community website which aims to make heritage accessible, through allowing users to share their community archives. You can explore West Yorkshire through the experiences of those who have lived there and explore photos and memories on topics including sport, festivals, shopping, religion, education and food.

You can search by keyword, but the 'topic' section is a good place to begin, as this gives a good flavour of the available material. There are over 120 information pages for Leeds history, with everything from shopping in the Leeds arcades to memories of the earliest Chapeltown carnivals. Although this site is strongest on history within living memory, this is an interesting project and a great way of seeing history through the eyes of those who were there.

Origins

www.origins.net: This is a pay per view website (which you can access free in the Leeds L&FH Library) which gives access to resources for British, Irish and Scottish family history, including wills, marriages and ship passenger lists.

The Luddite Link

http://ludditelink.org.uk: An information site created to commemorate the bicentenary of the Luddites in Yorkshire, the Luddite Link tells the story of the Luddite movement in the county. The Luddite protest movement began in the early 1800s in response to an increase in the use of machinery, particularly in the textiles industry which was such a huge employer in West Yorkshire. At this early stage, many textile workers were operating from their own homes and feared a loss of work through mechanisation.

The website has a section dedicated to the history of the Luddites and there is also an events section which profiles talks, lectures and other events related to the topic. You can view a timeline of Luddism and read papers by local historians. The 'partners & resources' section has a helpful list of which archives and libraries hold material relating to the movement and those who were involved in Luddite activities.

Tracks in Time
www.tracksintime.wyjs.org.uk: An online project from the West Yorkshire Archive Service, this aims to conserve, capture digitally and provide free online access to the historic tithe maps which cover the modern-day Leeds Metropolitan District, a huge area of ten large towns, from Wetherby in the north to Morley and Rothwell in the south.

Each of these tithe maps was originally a document used by diocesan and parish officials in the nineteenth century. Each hand-drawn plan, along with its accompanying apportionment data, shows land ownership, land use and land occupancy in both urban and rural areas of the Leeds district at a time of huge social and industrial change.

You can use the tithe map tool to search by modern-day postcode and zoom into locations to identify areas ranging from a whole township to an individual plot, as well as comparing historic and modern land usage. By placing modern and historic maps side by side, you can easily compare changes to land usage, whilst the surname search allows you to find where an ancestor owned or occupied land, what that land was used for and who else lived in the neighbourhood.

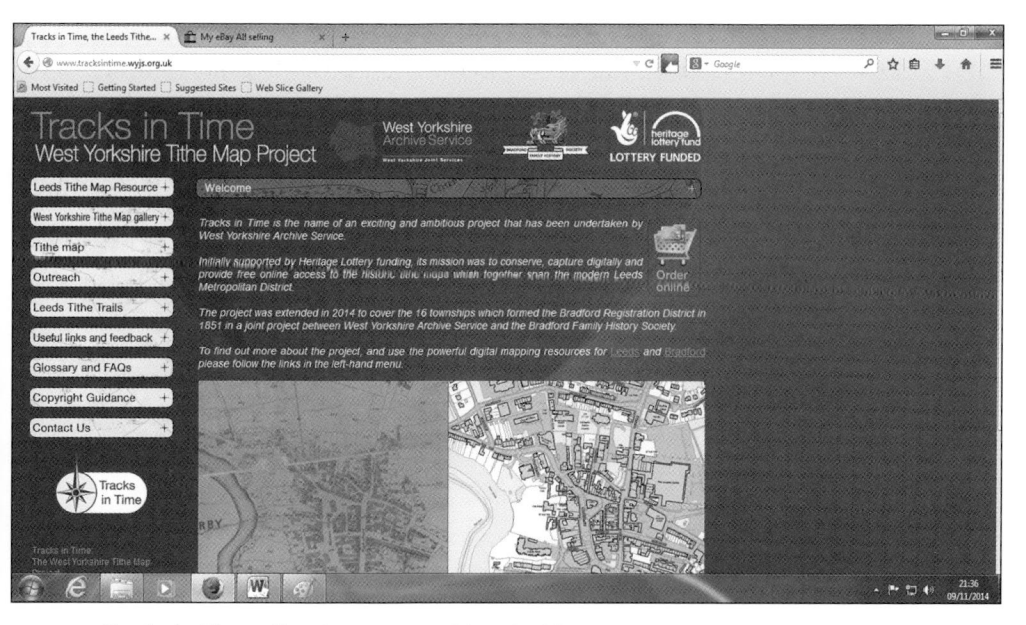

Tracks in Time offers free access to historic tithe maps.

The map gallery has thumbnail versions of each map in the collection which can be opened at full-screen size for detailed study, with the option to purchase if you wish. Whether you want to see how an area changed over time or to pinpoint a particular street, this is an invaluable resource that can be used in your own home.

Where is it in Yorkshire?
http://bit.ly/myleedswhere: The helpful 'Where is it in Yorkshire?' site is part of GENUKI Yorkshire which forms an index to all the place data on the main website. Simply select the first letter of the place you're searching for and you can then choose the location from an alphabetical list and click through to a page of information on your location, including churches in the area, background history, cemeteries, maps, schools, military records and probate records – most of which in turn link through to pages of further information.

Yorkshire BMD

www.yorkshirebmd.org.uk: The Yorkshire version of the BMD (births, marriages, deaths) website aims to make indexes to the county's birth, marriage and death records freely available online. The indexing is still ongoing and so this is a site worth checking regularly as more than five million Yorkshire records are already online.

The updates section is a good place to begin, as this lists the latest additions to the site, then you can choose to search by surname, adding in a forename or initial if you wish. Leeds is one of the regions available to choose as a geographical area once you have entered the surname you wish to search.

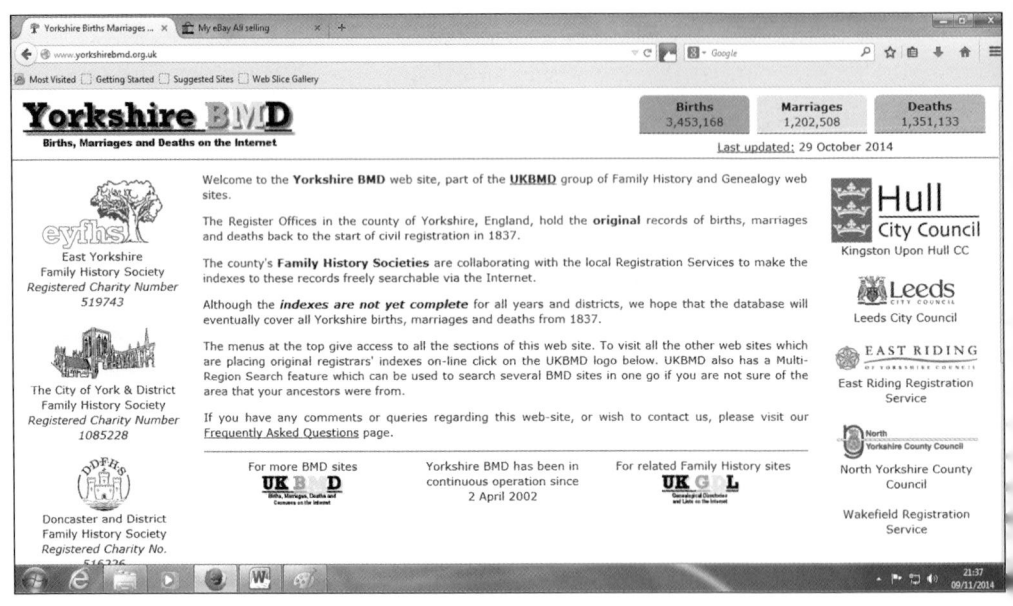

Yorkshire BMD has over five million Yorkshire records

Nineteenth-Century British Newspapers

http://bit.ly/myleedsnewspapers: An invaluable resource for Victorian (and slightly earlier) ancestors, British Newspapers is available via subscription or with a Leeds Library card. Here, you can search over two million pages of local and national newspapers, many of which have been selected by experts for their historic importance.

You can search via keywords, limiting the returned results to certain periods of time, or to selected newspapers. As with most online resources, the more specific you can be, the greater your chance of finding something of value. For a general search, the words 'woollen mill Leeds' brought up over forty records, including the sale of woollen mill machinery in March 1860 (in the *Leeds Mercury*), the letting of a four-storey mill at East Street in 1864 (*Leeds Mercury*) and details of an industrial accident which made the national headlines on 25 July 1869 in the *Lloyds Weekly Newspaper* when a boiler exploded at Berryoris Mill on Meadow Lane, when 'hundreds of windows were smashed at considerable distances' but fortunately there were no fatalities.

Births, deaths, marriages and obituaries are obviously of use for Leeds ancestors, as are details of properties changing hands, businesses opening and closing, and military news involving local regiments.

You can also save, bookmark, email and print out your results. The 'topic guide' has detailed information on using local and national newspapers for research, with advice on emigration, immigration, crime reports, sports reports and advertising. There are also helpful background guides on how our ancestors used newspapers, literacy rates, urban growth and Chartism.

Chapter 10

EXPLORE BYGONE LEEDS

So, you've trawled the internet, explored libraries and visited archives in your quest to discovery your ancestors. Now, it's time to take your research that extra step as we discover fascinating traces of bygone Leeds that you can explore today. There are two sections: walks and trails, and historic sites and visitor attractions.

If you aren't able to visit Leeds in person, the websites of many of the suggested sites have lots of interesting historical information, photos and in some cases, videos to enjoy instead.

So whatever the time of year and whatever stage your research is at, take a trip into the Leeds of days gone by.

Leeds Walks and Trails

Anglo Jewish Heritage Trail
Developed by Jewish historian Murray Freedman, the Leeds Anglo Jewish Heritage Trail is one of a network of trails across the UK which can be accessed via the trails website (www.jtrails.org.uk).

The trail begins at Briggate, where in the 1830s, jeweller Phineas Abrahams was one of the earliest Jewish traders in Leeds. Founder members of the Leeds Jewish community traded from plots running off Briggate, running businesses such as Marks & Spencers and Montague Burton, both of which have Jewish connections.

From here, you can take in the first two synagogues in Leeds – at the present day Merrion Centre and on Merrion Street, then the trail moves on to Vicar Lane, site of a tailoring workshop which belonged to Jewish tailor Herman Friend, one of the founders of large-scale tailoring in Leeds. Returning towards the centre of town, you can explore the site of clusters of Jewish shops of the 1940s and the

Brunswicks district, where better off members of the Jewish community lived.

Leeds Blue Plaque Scheme

Developed by the Leeds Civic Trust, the Blue Plaque Scheme was set up in 1987 to promote the heritage of the city and numbers 145 blue plaques around Leeds to date. These commemorate both people and buildings that have made a difference to life in the city. The first plaque was dedicated to 1950s track cyclist Beryl Burton OBE who lived in Morley and was twice a Road Racing World Champion. Other people commemorated are 'factory king' Richard Oastler who was born in St Peter's Square and wrote to the *Leeds Mercury* about factory slavery, beginning a country-wide campaign; and surgeon William Hey who lived on Albion Place and was one of the founders of Leeds General Infirmary.

If you'd like to tour some or all of the Leeds Blue Plaques you can see the list at the Open Plaques website (http://bit.ly/myleedsblueplaques). Many of the plaques are in central Leeds, including Park Row, Albion Place and Boar Lane, whilst others are further afield in historic centres of trade and industry including Armley and Morley. The Leeds Civic Trust bookshop on Wharf Street has a blue plaque guidebook for sale (http://bit.ly/myleedsctbookshop).

The Trust also runs regular guided walks around the city – these are a great way to soak up some history in the company of a volunteer with a real passion for Leeds and its past.

Leeds Industrial Heritage Trail

Leeds City Council's Industrial Heritage Trail is available from Leeds Tourist Information Centre next to the railway station and offers an introduction to how the city's industries have developed, through a walk around the city which you can either do all at once or pick and choose your own areas of interest.

The city centre area of the trail begins on Wellington Place, at the site of the former Bean Ing Mill, the world's first integrated woollen mill, where all of the process for turning raw wool into cloth took place under one roof. From here, you can move on to Leeds City Museum (originally a Mechanics Institute), Park Square (where

Park Square is one of the locations on the Industrial Heritage Trail © M Taylor.

some of the city's wealthiest Georgian residents once lived) and Thwaite Mills, where woollen cloth was produced as early as the seventeenth century.

To download the trail, visit: http://bit.ly/myleedsheritagetrail.

Leeds Owl Trail

The Leeds Owl Trail ® (www.leedsowltrail.com) was set up by artists interested in using the city's owl symbol as a way of seeing the city. The trail helps locals and visitors alike to enjoy the city's heritage – past and present – through following an 'owl walk' made up of old and new model or statue owls. The owl on the city's coat of arms was taken from the coat of arms of Sir John Savile, the city's first alderman.

The Owl Trail website has the trail in full and you can also pick up a leaflet with a map at Leeds Tourist Information Centre. The website also shows 'lost owls' which once featured on buildings that have now been demolished, including the Theatre Royal on Albion Street and a line of owls which stood on Monk Bridge until the 1930s.

The trail itself features twenty-five different owls, ten of which are in the city centre and fifteen a little further afield, but still within walking distance. The trail begins in Millennium Square with owl statues created to provide work in the Great Depression of the 1930s,

The city's owl symbol inspired the Leeds Owl Trail © Leeds Owl Trail.

moving through buildings including the Leeds City Museum and the owls of the Old Leeds School Board. Each owl has its own potted history as part of the trail and this is an interesting way to learn more about the city, particularly in the Victorian era.

Leeds Tithe Trails
A legacy of Tracks in Time (http://www.tracksintime.wyjs.org.uk), the West Yorkshire Tithe Map Project Tithe Trails is a set of six different walks which allow you to discover the heritage of different areas of the city, many of which have changed greatly over the past two centuries, as the tithe maps themselves show.

The trails, which can be downloaded from the website, are: Armley/Bramley, Beeston/Holbeck, Calverley/Horsforth, Headingley/Armley, Pudsey/Tong and Wetherby/Linton. These include clear and detailed walk descriptions, along with photographs of landmarks you'll find along the way, and points of historic interest along the trail.

Each trail also includes an image of the relevant tithe map. The Holbeck/Beeston trail makes a good starting point, as this is one of the shorter walks, at 1.5 miles, and covers both streets and parkland. It begins in the historic townships of Holbeck and follows the tithe boundary with Beeston as far as possible. Along the way you'll visit Holbeck Cemetery (with burials including former Leeds mayor Henry Rowland Marsden and local poet Tony Harrison), part of the track of the Middleton Railway and Cross Flats Park, a local landmark which was one of the few areas of Leeds to be heavily bombed in the Second World War.

Potts Clocks Heritage Trail
www.leedsinspired.co.uk/events/potts-clocks-heritage-trail:
Following a similar format to the Leeds Owl Trail, the Potts Clocks trail covers five generations of clock making in Leeds by the Potts family firm, who have made over 1,600 clocks for public buildings around the world.

William Potts & Sons was founded by William Potts, an apprentice clockmaker who, in 1833, set up his own business in Pudsey. He began by repairing clocks but gradually expanded to create his own timepieces and by 1862 had premises in the city centre. The firm produced clocks for some of the city's most famous Victorian buildings, including the Town Hall and the Corn Exchange. The company was granted a Royal Warrant in 1897 and produced clocks for public buildings around the country, with William's three sons joining the family business.

Leeds Visitor Centre, Leeds Town Hall and Leeds Library all have trail maps and the whole walk lasts around ninety minutes, taking in landmark buildings including the Town Hall, Leeds Minster and the Old Post Office.

The Leeds Heritage Trail
Developed by the Leeds Civic Trust (www.leedscivictrust.org.uk), the Leeds Heritage Trail is a series of city walks based on twelve different themes with quirky titles including 'Ale, arms, Aire and Calder', 'On Tenterhooks' and 'Arcadian delights'.

To follow the trails, you can purchase the book from Leeds Civic Trust which has 3D maps and over 400 photographs.

Walking Through Our History Heritage Trail
http://marksintime.marksandspencer.com: As Leeds is the city where Marks & Spencer started trading, the company is proud of its roots and has recently developed a heritage walking trail in partnership with the University of Leeds and the Leeds City Council Library Service. The trail begins, appropriately enough, at the little market stall at Kirkgate Market where the company began training with the words 'Don't ask the price, it's a penny!'

You can also explore other key sites including the company's first store at the Cross Arcade in the city centre and one of Leeds's oldest streets, Briggate, which was built in 1207 and by the Victorian era was a wide and busy road with shops along its length. Arcades and theatres were built alongside and Briggate's first M&S store opened in 1909. The trail ends at the Marks & Spencer Archive at the University of Leeds where you can explore some of the 70,000 items in the collections and view a permanent exhibition on the history of M&S and shopping in Britain.

Historic Sites and Visitor Attractions

The Leeds Tapestry

The beautiful Victorian Central Library beside the Town Hall is home to the Leeds Local & Family History Library. The entrance hall and stairways of the buildings are an architectural treat in themselves, and it is fascinating to imagine how awed our ancestors must have felt when part of the building was the town's 'public free library'. On floor one is the Leeds Tapestry, a collection of sixteen tapestries which celebrate the history and diversity of the city and were created by different Leeds communities.

The tapestry can be viewed at any time during library opening hours and its themes include industrial heritage, the environment, transport, education and health.

This work of art took ten years to create and was completed in 2002. You can enrich your viewing of the tapestry by asking at the information desk for one of the tapestry volunteers to talk to you about it.

Discovery Centre

The Discovery Centre is a state of the art resource and storage facility for over one million items which are cared for by Leeds Museums. The Centre is located close to the city's Royal Armouries Museum and visitors are welcome by appointment. As only up to 10 per cent of the city's museum collections are displayed in its museums at any one time, this is a great way to find out more about the items not currently on public view.

The collections are strong on social and industrial history, with examples of textile and printing machinery, as well as holdings from companies including John Fowler & Co., Vickers PLC, Benjamin Gott, Burtons and Kirkstall Forge.

Staff are in the process of evaluating the collections fully and over the coming years, will look to make more of this material available to the public. In the meantime, they are happy to answer queries about the material the Centre holds, as an online catalogue is still some way off at the time of going to press.

Discovery Centre, Carlisle Road, Leeds LS10 1LB; tel.: 0113 378 2100; email: discovery.centre@leeds.gov.uk; website: http://bit.ly/myleedsdc

Explore Bygone Leeds

The Leeds Waterfront

Visit the place which made Leeds an inland port, when the River Aire was made navigable from Leeds Bridge through to the east coast in 1700 and the Leeds and Liverpool was opened in 1816. This combined waterway system gave access to the ports of Hull in the east and Liverpool in the west, offering Leeds traders the possibility of trading not only with these ports, but with mainland Europe and the Americas.

Leeds Civic Trust (www.leedscivictrust.org.uk) runs Waterfront guided walks a few times a year and you can also explore the area yourself using the information boards in the area to guide you.

The Leeds Liverpool Canal was one of the main reasons for the growth of the town in the eighteenth century.

The north of the river is where the first medieval mills appeared and wool was cleaned and fulled. Further downriver, Leeds Bridge is on the site of one of the earliest crossing points of the River Aire in Leeds, and close to Leeds Parish Church, a Victorian church which stands on a site that has been a place of Christian worship for over 1,000 years.

Middleton Railway
A heritage railway with over 250 years of history, Middleton Railway was established in 1758 and today's passengers can experience a steam-train ride on what is claimed to be the world's oldest railway. You can see an exhibition which introduces the history of the railway, showing its links to the locomotive building industry that grew up in South Leeds. Steam, diesel and electric locomotives are on display, including a Cockerill 1625 built in 1890, a Manning Wardle 1210 from the year 1881 and a 1933 Kitson 5469.

The nearby woodland has traces of the ancient coal mining industry with bell pits, where the coal was dug out before coal mines were established.

Middleton Railway, The Station, Moor Road, Hunslet, Leeds LS10 2JQ; tel.: 0845 680 1758; email: info@middletonrailway.org.uk; website: www.middletonrailway.org.uk

Hyde Park Picture House
One of the country's oldest cinemas, Hyde Park Picture House celebrated its centenary in 2014 and is a listed building just outside the city centre. The cinema opened on 7 November 1914, in the early months of the First World War, with a debut showing of the patriotic drama *Their Only Son*. The cinema has lasted through the advent of the 'talkies', the threat from television and, finally, the growing popularity of multi-screen cinemas in the 1980s and 1990s. It was saved from demolition in 1989 when Leeds City Council stepped in to prevent its closure.

The grade II listed building has many original features including functional gas lighting, an ornate balcony and a piano, which would have provided the sound for silent film showings. The cinema is billed as 'the cosiest cinema in Leeds' and cinema goers can still see a programme of independent, art house and classic films every week. *Hyde Park Picture House, 73 Brudenell Road, Leeds LS6 1JD; tel.: 0113 275 2045; email: info@hydeparkpicturehouse.co.uk; website: www.hydeparkpicturehouse.co.uk*

Kirkgate Market
A trip to Europe's largest indoor market gives a great insight into the shopping experiences of our Victorian and early twentieth-century ancestors. Both the food and non-food markets have stalls which have been in the same family for generations, and the bustling atmosphere has changed little over the decades.

Look above eye level at the fantastic glass roof and ornate

Kirkgate Market is considered one of the finest historic market halls in Europe.

ironwork which must have appeared amazing to our ancestors, who were more used to corner shops and small open-air markets. Monthly tours of the market are available: phone or ask at the market's visitor centre for details.

Several Leeds suburbs also have atmospheric markets, including Morley, Yeadon and Pudsey.

Kirkgate Market, Vicar Lane, Leeds LS2 7HY; tel.: 0113 378 1950; website: www.leedsmarkets.co.uk/m/kirkgate-market

Dark Arches

A marvel of Victorian engineering far below Leeds Railway Station, the Dark Arches is a complex of brick tunnels. In the 1860s, more than eighteen million bricks were used to create the tunnel complex, through which the River Aire flows, with access also to the Leeds/Liverpool canal. The vast area is still one of the world's largest underground structures and beyond the tunnels is Granary Wharf, a complex of shops and restaurants, where you can see old waterways machinery on the canal. *www.granarywharf.co.uk*

The Corn Exchange

The Corn Exchange is one of the city's landmark Victorian buildings and stands close to the heart of old Leeds, with Leeds Parish Church and the city's first Cloth Halls nearby. The Corn Exchange was built in 1863 after a design by Cuthbert Brodick and is a grade I listed structure. As the name suggests, this was a trading centre for corn, and is now one of only three such exchanges in the country which is still used for trading (albeit not corn).

Nowadays, the Corn Exchange is home to a number of independent shops and cafes, as well as community initiatives such as dance lessons. The building has been superbly restored and visitors can enjoy its grandeur both from ground level and the upper arcades.

Corn Exchange, Call Lane, Leeds LS1 7BR; tel.: 0113 234 0363; website: www.leedscornexchange.co.uk

Heritage Open Days

Look out for the Heritage Open Days Festival (www.heritageopen

The Corn Exchange is close to the heart of old Leeds.

days.org.uk) which takes place every September at sites across the UK. The idea of the festival is to give members of the public the chance to visit buildings which aren't normally open to the public, or to give behind the scenes access to areas of public buildings which are normally restricted.

Events include walks, talks, demonstrations, lectures, guided tours and workshop sessions. Among the participants in Leeds are churches, graveyards, markets, Leeds Town Hall, Leeds Museums, the Leeds Civic Trust, Marks & Spencer Archive and Leeds University.

The website allows you to search for an event by keyword or region and there is also an 'if you like this...' option to show you similar events in your area.

Leeds Industrial Museum

A museum of industrial heritage housed in what was one of the world's largest woollen mills, Armley Mills. Visitors can explore the mill buildings, which are full of exhibits relating to textiles, clothing, printing, engineering and locomotive building in Leeds. Among the highlights of the collections are the working locomotive *Jack* which, on selected days, takes passengers along the museum's train track; and one of the world's smallest operating 1920s cinemas.

The museum runs a regular programme of events and exhibitions.

Leeds Industrial Museum, Canal Road, Armley Leeds LS12 2QF; tel.: 0113 378 3173; email: armley.mills@leeds.gov.uk; website: bit.ly/myleedsarmley

Leeds Minster

Leeds Minster (also known as Leeds Parish Church) is important not only for its place in the religious history of the city, but also for the fact that it stands on the site of the area where life in Leeds began. The church is close to the banks of the River Aire, at one of the river's first ever crossing points.

The present church opened in 1841 and stands on the site of several former churches, the earliest known of which dates back to at least the seventh century. The church contains several important

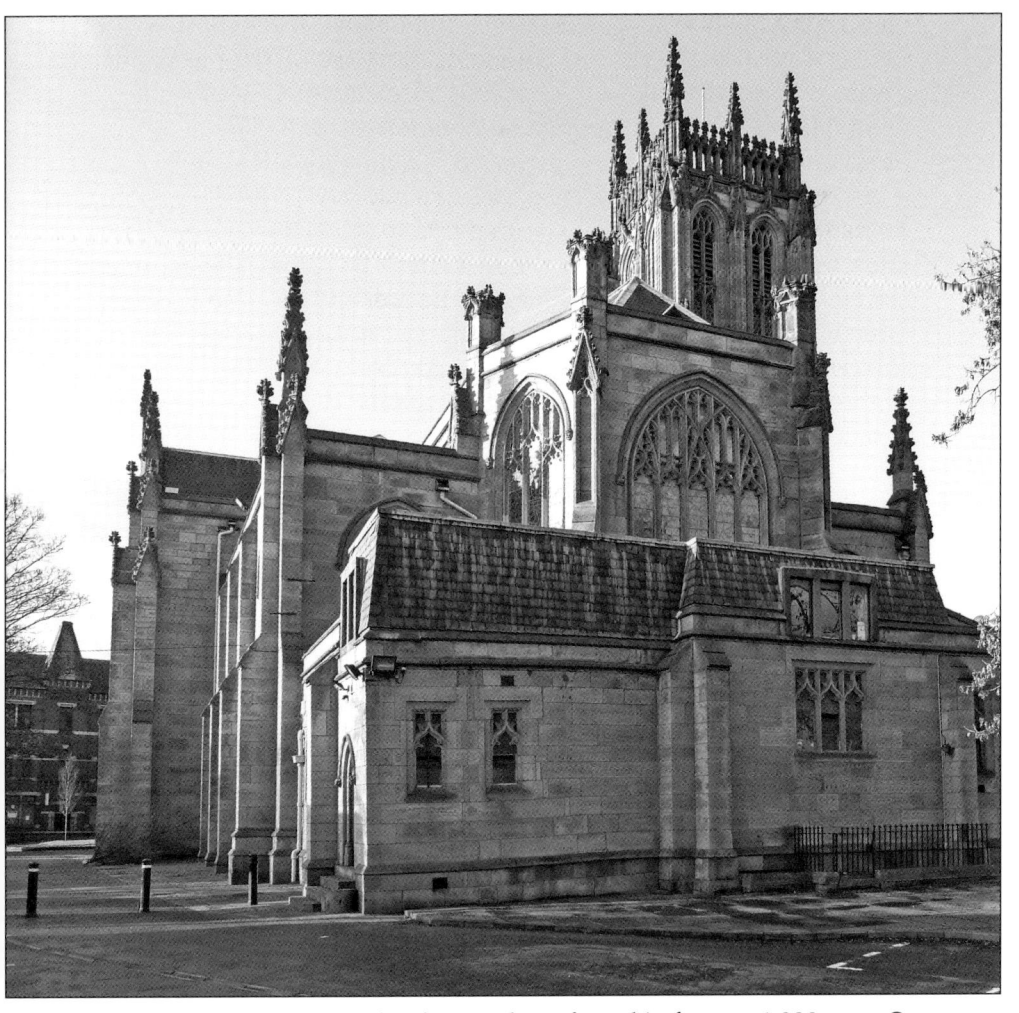

The site of Leeds Minister has been a place of worship for over 1,000 years © Tim Green.

memorials including a brass work which commemorates Captain Oates's Antarctic expedition as well as monuments to important Leeds families including the Lodge family, Cooksons, Milners and Fentons. The Minster is also home to the Leeds Cross, a tenth-

century Anglo-Scandinavian stone cross which is one of the city's oldest surviving objects. The Minster's archives are kept at WYAS Leeds.
Leeds Minster, Kirkgate, Leeds LS2 7DJ; tel.: 0113 245 2036; email: contact@leedsminster.org; website: www.leedsminster.org

Lotherton Hall
An Edwardian country house run by Leeds City Council, which was once home to the Gascoigne family. The hall and its grounds show what it was like to live and work on a large rural estate at the turn of the twentieth century. Collections on display in the house include pottery, porcelain, furniture and costumes, and the exhibition programme profiles life both above and below stairs. The Hall's archives are kept by WYAS Leeds.
Lotherton Hall, Aberford, Leeds LS25 3EB; tel.: 0113 281 3259; website: bit.ly/myleedslotherton

Chapter 11

LEEDS DIRECTORY

This chapter brings together contact details for the many libraries, museums, archives and societies which can be of help to you during your quest to discover your Leeds ancestors.

In most cases, archives require you to make an appointment and bring along ID before visiting. If you'd like to see specific archive material at a library or museum, it is always worth checking beforehand in case an appointment is needed.

All contact details are correct at the time of going to press. You are advised to check details with the organisation before visiting.

Leeds Local and Family History Societies
If you've been inspired by delving into the history of Leeds, have hit a brick wall in your research or would simply like to find out more about life in the city in days gone by, consider joining one or more of these societies.

Many hold regular meetings in the city, with lectures, talks, walks and trips, and most publish a regular newsletter with information on the newest research relating to Leeds.

East Leeds History & Archaeology Society
A group which promotes the history and archaeology of the eastern area of the city. The society was founded in 1997 and since then members have enjoyed lectures, displays and have organised a twice-yearly publication programme. The group's home is the East Leeds Heritage Centre in Crossgates where displays and exhibitions are staged regularly. Membership is £8 per year/£40 life membership. *Membership Secretary, ELHAS, 16 Manston Drive, Crossgates, Leeds LS15 8RA; website: www.elhas.org.uk*

Friends of Beckett Street Cemetery recently celebrated its thirtieth anniversary.

Friends of Beckett Street Cemetery
Founded in 1984, when the Victorian cemetery Beckett Street was threatened with closure, Friends of Beckett Cemetery liaises with Leeds City Council to safeguard the future of this historic burial ground and also organises meetings, walks and working groups to help maintain the cemetery. Members receive a regular newsletter and can attend all meetings and the AGM.
http://beckettstreetcemetery.org.uk

Friends of Holbeck Cemetery
Founded in 2001, this community group works to protect and conserve the Victorian era Holbeck Cemetery, which was opened in 1857 and stands high above Leeds, with views over the city and

beyond towards Bradford and Shipley. Among those buried here are Victorian industrialists and inventors, former Lord Mayors of Leeds, William Gott (the older brother of textile pioneer Benjamin Gott) and – perhaps the best known – Henry Rowland Marsden, a Holbeck born man who made his fortune in the USA and returned home to become Mayor of Leeds.

The Friends group conducts tours and walks for schoolchildren, young adults and members of the public, as well as carrying out outreach work and organising local and national talks and presentations.

For more information on the group, contact Eve and Ken Tidswell, tel.: 0113 277 2403; email: roops73@aol.com

Friends of Holbeck Cemetery works to protect the historic burial ground.

Members of Friends of Lawnswood Cemetery on one of their recent action days.

Friends of Lawnswood Cemetery

A society established in 2011 to protect and promote Lawnswood Cemetery for future generations. This ten-acre burial ground was established in Victorian times at Rawdon on the outskirts of Leeds. The group holds 'action days' on the first Saturday of each month, when volunteers undertake various maintenance tasks at the cemetery, and regular guided walks are held during the summer months.
For details, visit: http://friendsoflawnswoodcemetery.co.uk/

Friends of Leeds Museums

For over forty years, this Friends group has worked to 'support and assist' the Leeds Museums, with a programme of exhibitions, lectures and outdoor activities, as well as fundraising campaigns which, over the decades, have brought or kept important historical items within the Leeds Museums.

Most recently, the group helped to keep the West Yorkshire Hoard in Leeds, along with the help of other local heritage groups and public donations. This important collection of Anglo-Saxon jewellery is now in storage and will eventually go on permanent display in the city.

New members are always welcome and enjoy free admission to a range of museums across the city, as well as visits, social events and a regular newsletter.

For more information, contact the group's chairman Dr John Pearson (email: jspearsonster@googlemail.com) or visit: http://friendsofleedsmuseums.org

Garforth Historical Society

An active society open to anyone with an interest in the history of the Garforth area of Leeds. Members meet monthly for talks on various aspects of the area's past and also work on local history projects, the most recent being a survey of the churchyard of St Mary the Virgin in Garforth. The results of the survey's findings are available on the society's website and here you can also find a historic walk to follow, articles and photos relating to the area's past and details of upcoming events.

For more information, visit: www.garforthhistoricalsociety.org.uk

Jewish Genealogical Society of Great Britain

A national genealogical society for anyone with Jewish ancestors. The society has a Leeds branch. However, as officers are in the process of changing roles, researchers are requested to contact the branch via the main society contacts. Members can access a London library of over 1,000 Jewish geneaology books, attend regional meetings, search 'members only' genealogy lists online and attend conferences and workshops.

Jewish Geneaological Society of Great Britain, 33 Seymour Place, London W1H 5AU; tel.: 0207 724 4232; email: enquiries@jgsgb.org.uk; website: www.jgsgb.org.uk

Leeds Irish Historical & Cultural Society
A society established in 2002 for those interested in the history and culture of Irish communities in Leeds. The society aims to create an oral history archive, encourage family history research and to campaign for the preservation and restoration of Mount St Mary's Church, built specifically for Irish families who fled the Irish famine. *For more information, email: info@lichs.org.uk; website: www.lichs.org.uk*

Morley Local History Society
Founded in 1965, in the days when Morley was a burgh, the society covers Morley and the surrounding areas of Churwell, Gildersome, Drighlington, East Ardsley and West Ardsley. Members meet monthly between September and April and also receive a regular newsletter. The group carries out research projects, and most recently completed a study of the Co-operative Society in Morley.

Membership is £8.50 per year and you can find out more at the group's website: www.morleylhs.btck.co.uk

North West Catholic History Society
A society which exists to promote the study of the history of Catholicism in the northwest of England and to publish material relating to Catholic history. The society also produces an annual research journal.
Join Morley Local History Society for regular meetings on the history of this ancient town. © Morley Local History Society

North West Catholic History Society, c/o Mr J Hilton, 282 Whelley, Wigan WN2 1DA; www.catholic-history.org.uk/nwchs

Pudsey Civic Society

Covering a wide area including Calverley, Farsley, Stanningley, Rodley and Fulneck, Pudsey Civic Society promotes the conservation and heritage of the former burgh of Pudsey. The group's local and family history collection is an impressive holding of more than 10,000 items, many of which have been donated by people local to the Pudsey area. The collection is kept at Pudsey Library and members are working on indexing the collection for future online searching. Items include old photographs, books, newspapers, monumental inscriptions and maps.

Members attend talks in the winter months and can take part in walks during the summer. The group also plays an active part in local life by keeping an eye on planning applications and new building developments, making their views known to the local authorities where applicable.

Membership Secretary, Pudsey Civic Society, PO Box 146, Leeds LS28 8WY; website: www.pcs-online.org.uk

Thoresby Society

A historical society for Leeds and surrounding areas, open to anyone with an interest in the history of the city and its development over the years. The society has its own library and archives, both of which are open to members, and members also receive the society's free annual publication.

Members meet for monthly talks and attend summer excursions. The group's website has useful resources available to non-members, including a Leeds

Ralph Thoresby (1658-1925), the first Leeds historian, after whom the Thoresby Society is named (image from The Story of Leeds by JS Fletcher).

timeline, an account of the man after whom the group is named – historian Ralph Thoresby – as well as articles and photographs.
Thoresby Society, 23 Clarendon Road, Leeds LS2 9NZ; tel.: 0113 247 0704; email: secretary@thoresby.org.uk; website: www.thoresby.org.uk

Victorian Society West Yorkshire Group
A regional society of the UK-wide Victorian Society, this West Yorkshire Group organises member talks, walks and visits, as well as helping to raise awareness of Victorian buildings which are in need of restoration or are in danger of being demolished or damaged.
For details, contact Stephen Walker, Roundwood Grange, Roundwood Road, Baildon, Shipley, W Yorks BD17 7JX; tel.: 01274 586065; email: Stephen.walker34@btopenworld.com; website: www.victoriansocietyorg.uk

Yorkshire Archaeological Society
Despite its county-wide title, the Yorkshire Archaeological Society has plenty to offer researchers interested in Leeds rather than the whole of Yorkshire, with the added bonus of its archives and library being based in central Leeds, behind the Town Hall.

The library covers topics including local, social and industrial history, as well as place names and heraldry.

Family history resources include microfiches of parish registers, the GRO index and indexes to wills. In the archives are family archives, maps, wills and manorial court rolls. Staff are currently indexing all collections held in the archives, with a view to making these available online. Until then, some of the holdings are listed on the Access to Archives and WYAS websites.
Yorkshire Archaeological Society, 25 Clarendon Road, Leeds LS2 9NZ; tel.: 0113 245 7910; email: yas.enquiries@gmail.com; website: www.yas.org.uk

Archives

John Goodchild Collection
A large local history collection which centres on Wakefield and which is kept at WYAS Wakefield (although independently of this

archive), the John Goodchild Collection contains material relating to the Central West Riding, including Leeds. The material dates from the twelfth century onwards and is particularly strong on eighteenth- and nineteenth-century material. There are over 1,000 boxes of manuscripts on the history of people and institutions of the West Riding over the centuries, as well as books, maps and illustrations.

The collection's keeper, John Goodchild, has been a collector since the 1960s and, over the years, a myriad of individuals and organisations have gifted material to the collection, knowing that it will be preserved for the future and enjoyed by historians. Donors include solicitors, booksellers, surveyors and business owners. Further material has come via auction, second hand bookshops and derelict premises.

John Goodchild has written over 100 books and essays and is happy for members of the public to access the archives by appointment. The collection is card-indexed, and its complexity is reflected in the fact that it comprises tens of thousands of index cards, with more detailed listings for in-depth subjects.
John Goodchild Collection, WYAS Wakefield, Newstead Road, Wakefield WF1 2DE; tel.: 01924 306809

Leeds Diocesan Archives
The main archive repository for Leeds Roman Catholic ancestors, with school records, parish magazines, church newspapers, photographs and also archive items relating to the city's Roman Catholic Cathedral, St Anne's.
Leeds Diocesan Archives, Hinsley Hall, 62 Headingley Lane, Leeds LS6 2BX; tel.: 0113 261 8031; email: robert.finnigan@dioceseofleeds.org.uk; website: www.dioceseofleeds.org.uk/archives

Leeds University Special Collections
The Leeds University Library Special Collections holds some of the finest and rarest books in the country. There are over 200,000 books and hundreds of thousands of manuscripts in the collections. Items of interest to family historians include material donated by the Quaker Library and the Yorkshire Collection, with biographies of

Leeds University Library welcomes more than two million visitors each year. © Tim Green

eminent Yorkshire people, books about local and church history and old guidebooks.

The Special Collections website gives access to an archive blog, which includes regularly updated news of various accessions. *Department of Special Collections, University of Leeds, Leeds LS2 9JT; tel.: 0113 343 5518; http://library.leeds.ac.uk/special-collections; email: specialcollections@library.leeds.ac.uk*

M&S Company Archives

Based at the University of Leeds, this specialist archive tells the story of over 100 years of retailing, starting with a small stall in Kirkgate Market through to a global chain of stores. The archive comprises

more than 70,000 items including staff magazines, advertising material, company memorabilia, photographs, film, oral history and the company's past packaging and advertising material.
M&S Company Archives, University of Leeds, Leeds LS2 9JT; tel.: 0208 8718 2800; website:https://marksintime.marksandspencer.com/the-collection; email: companyarchive@marks-and-spencer.com

The Romany Collection
Part of the Leeds University Libraries Special Collection, the Romany Collection is one of the few specialist collections in the UK devoted to Romany history. The collection covers both gypsies and related traveller groups and includes books, notebooks relating to tales told by travellers, classic printed works on British and European gypsies, and photographs.
The Romany Collection, Department of Special Collections, University of Leeds, Leeds LS2 9JT; tel.: 0113 343 5518; http://library.leeds.ac.uk/special-collections; email: specialcollections@library.leeds.ac.uk

West Yorkshire Archive Service Leeds
The city's main archive repository and part of the West Yorkshire-wide network which also has offices in Bradford, Calderdale, Kirklees and Calderdale. The Leeds WYAS is located in Morley, four miles from the city centre. Here, you can access a huge range of

The Leeds office of West Yorkshire Archive Service. © David Weston

business, industrial, council and social records. The WYAS website has a helpful starting point (http://www.archives.wyjs.org.uk/archives-our-collections.asp) where you can explore the collections, then decide where to start your research.
West Yorkshire Archives Service Leeds, Nepshaw Lane South, Morley, Leeds, LS27 7JQ; tel.: 0113 393 9788; email: leeds@wyjs.org.uk; website: www.archives.wyjs.org.uk/archives-leeds.asp

West Yorkshire Archive Service Wakefield
Four miles from central Leeds, WYAS Wakefield is home to Quarter Session records and the Registry of Deeds.
West Yorkshire Archives Service Wakefield, Newstead Road, Wakefield WF1 2DE; tel.: 01924 305980; email: wakefield@wyjs.org.uk; website: http://bit.ly/myleedswyasw

Yorkshire Film Archive
With more than 500 items relating to life in bygone Leeds, the Yorkshire Film Archive is a great way to look at the city's history in a different way. The archive comprises more than a century of film archive, beginning with the first known moving film footage (shot in Leeds in 1888 by Louise le Prince) through to more modern footage relating to festivals, parades and demonstrations.

Many of the films are available to view online and you can search by keyword or place name.
Yorkshire Film Archive, York St John College, Lord Mayors Walk, York YO31 7EX; tel.: 01904 876550; email: yfa@yorksj.ac.uk; website: yorkshirefilmarchive.com

Libraries

Brotherton Library
A library on the main campus of Leeds University which is home to the University's Special Collections comprising over 200,000 books and hundreds of rare documents. The collections are particularly strong on business, education, the history of Yorkshire and religion.
Brotherton Library, University of Leeds, Leeds LS2 9JT; tel.: 0113 343 5518; email: specialcollections@library.leeds.ac.uk; website: http://library.leeds.ac.uk/special-collection

Leeds Directory

Leeds Local and Family History Library
The city's central library, next to the Town Hall, is home to the Leeds Local & Family History Library. Located on the second floor of a grand Victorian building, the library has a beautiful reading and study room, computer facilities and a help desk for enquiries. There are more than 180,000 items on local and family history for Leeds, including books, journals, photos, maps, trade directories and prints and microfilms.
Local and Family History Library, Leeds Central Library, Calverley Street, Leeds LS1 3AB; tel.: 0113 247 8290; email: local&familyhistory@leeds.gov.uk; website: www.leeds.gov.uk/localandfamilyhistory

Leeds City Libraries
Leeds Central Library, home to the Leeds Local & Family History Library, is the city's largest public library. Leeds City Libraries comprises a total of thirty-six libraries, from suburbs close to the city (such as Headingley and Armley) to further afield locations within the Leeds district, including Otley and Wetherby.

   At each of these libraries members can enjoy free internet access and borrow up to twenty books. The branch libraries hold copies of local interest and local history books which are specific to that particular area.
For a full list of libraries and their contact details, visit: http://www.leeds.gov.uk/leisure/Pages/Your-library.aspx

Leeds Library
Founded in 1768 as a subscription library, the Leeds Library is one of the oldest libraries of its kind. Around 1,500 new books and periodicals are added each year and there are several important collections which are valuable to family history researchers including topography, Civil War pamphlets and volumes relating to the history of Yorkshire families.

   The library is open six days a week (closed on Sundays) and staff run regular tours where you can find out more about the collections.
18 Commercial Street, Leeds LS1 6AL; tel.: 0113 245 3071; email: enquiries@theleedslibrary.org.uk; website: www.theleedslibrary.org.uk

Leeds University Library

One of the UK's major research libraries which has extensive manuscript, print and online collections gathered during the course of a century. You don't have to be a student at the university to visit; more than two million visitors go along each year. The most important resource for anyone researching Leeds ancestors is the library's Special Collections, which are referred to throughout this book.

Leeds University Library, University of Leeds, Leeds LS2 9JT; tel.: 0113 343 5663; website: http://library.leeds.ac.uk

Museums

Middleton Railway

The home of the world's continuously operating railway, Middleton Railway is a heritage railway with a museum which focuses on the locomotive industry in Leeds, with plenty of historic locomotives to see.

Middleton Railway, Moor Road Railway Station, Leeds LS10 2JQ; tel.: 0113 271 0320; website: www.middletonrailway.org.uk

Leeds Museums Discovery Centre

The Discovery Centre cares for the collections of all of the Leeds Museums and is home to more than a million historic items. Visitors are welcome by appointment and the centre runs regular 'behind the scenes' tours.

Leeds Museums Discovery Centre, Carlisle Road, Leeds LS10 1LB; tel.: 0113 378 2100; website: www.leeds.gov.uk/museumsandgalleries/ Pages/discoverycentre.aspx

Kirkstall Abbey and Abbey House Museum

Visit the medieval Cistercian monastery which was one of the earliest cloth producers in the Leeds area. The Abbey ruins are substantial and the visitor centre helps to put the remaining buildings into context.

Across the road is Abbey House Museum, a museum devoted to the city's history, with recreated Victorian streets, houses and shops, as well as displays of local memorabilia.

Leeds Directory

Kirkstall Abbey, Abbey Road, Leeds LS5 3EH; tel.: 0113 230 5492; website: www.leeds.gov.uk/museumsandgalleries/Pages/Kirkstall-Abbey.aspx
Abbey House Museum, Abbey Walk, Leeds LS5 3EH;
tel.: 0113 230 5492; website: www.leeds.gov.uk/museumsandgalleries/Pages/Abbey-House-Museum.aspx

Leeds City Museum

Four floors of Leeds history, from prehistoric times through to the present day. Leeds City Museum is a family-friendly museum with displays which include Victorian Leeds, textiles, industry, ancient Leeds and medieval Leeds.
Leeds City Museum, Millennium Square, Leeds LS2 8BH;
tel.: 0113 224 3732; website: www.leeds.gov.uk/museumsandgalleries/Pages/Leeds-City-Museum.aspx

Leeds Industrial Museum

Historic Armley Mills is home of the Leeds Industrial Museum where you can see authentic working machinery which brought the city to prominence during the Industrial Revolution.

Textiles, engineering, printing and locomotives are all covered and exhibits range from the eighteenth century through to the present day.
Leeds Industrial Museum, Canal Road, Leeds LS12 2QF;
tel.: 0113 263 7861; website: www.leeds.gov.uk/museumsandgalleries/Pages/armleymills.aspx

CONCLUSION

The great joy of family history research is that the search to find out more about your ancestors can be never ending. With so many resources available to us, tracing those who lived before us is an enjoyable pursuit that can occupy as few or as many hours as we wish.

The huge city of Leeds, with its diverse population, plethora of trades and huge range of leisure pursuits is a pleasure to explore, whether you're marvelling at the Victorian architecture of a splendid shopping arcade or unrolling historic maps to discover how an area changed over time. Whether knowingly or unwittingly, our Leeds ancestors, whoever they were, have left us many tantalising clues to their lives and it's our privilege and pleasure to solve this hugely fascinating puzzle.

READING LIST

Nick Barratt, *Tracing the History of Your House: A Guide to Sources* (Public Record Office, 2001)

Steven Bart and Kevin Brady, *The Illustrated History of Leeds* (Breedon Books, 2002)

WB Crump, *Leeds Woollen Industry: 1780–1820* (Thoresby Society, vol. 32; 1931)

Ann Heap, *The Headrow* (Leeds City Libraries, 1990)

Ann Heap and Peter Brears, *Leeds Described: Eye Witness Accounts of Leeds 1534–1905* (Breedon Books, 1993)

Clifford Lackey, *Quality Pays: The Story of Joshua Tetley & Son* (Springwood Books, 1985)

Malcolm Macdonald and Martin Jarred, *The Leeds United Story* (Breedon Books, 1992)

Percy Robinson, *Leeds Old and New* (Richard Jackson Ltd, 1926)

Brian Thompson, *Portrait of Leeds* (Robert Hall, 1971)

David Thornton, *The Story of Leeds* (History Press, 2013)

Ronald Wilkinson, *The Grand Theatre: The First 100 Years: 1878–1978* (Roger Iredale, 1977)

D Williams, *Leeds School Board and its Architecture: 1870–1903* (Leeds Polytechnic, 1975)

INDEX

Access to Archives, 19, 62
Armley Industrial Museum, 33
Baptists, 88–89
Boar Lane, 3
Briggate, 3, 4
Burton's Tailors, 32
Census, 20–1, 45, 68–9, 76, 114
Church of England, 79–81
Cinema, 105–8, 130–1
Civil War, 3
Education, 56–63
Immigration, 66–70
Islam, 90–1
Judaism, 91–4, 122–3, 141
Kirkgate, 3
Kirkstall Abbey, 3
Leeds Local & Family History Library, 11, 14–18, 22, 24, 35, 43–4, 48, 103–4, 105, 149
Leeds Museums, 35
Leeds University Special Collections, 24, 64–5, 145–6, 148
Leodis website, 38, 42, 51, 78, 96, 103, 108, 111–12, 115–16
Maps, 5, 17, 24–5, 44–5, 118–19, 126
Markets, 28, 47–49, 131–2
Medieval Leeds, 1, 2, 3

Methodism, 86–8
Middleton Railway, 34
Newspapers, 20, 21–2, 49, 64, 75–6, 95, 107, 120–1
Non-conformism, 81–94
Oral history, 69–70, 96
Parish registers, 24
Railways, 5, 6, 33–5, 130, 150
Registry of Deeds, 45–6
Religion, 79–94
River Aire, 1, 4, 28, 39, 46
Roman Catholicism, 83–6, 142, 145
Shopping, 48–51, 53–5
Sport, 95–8
Tetleys Breweries, 32–3
Textile trade, 3, 4, 10, 28–32, 67
Theatre, 100–5
Thoresby, Ralph, 4, 143
Thoresby Society, 19, 22, 24, 143
Title deeds, 42–3
Town Hall, 7, 8, 10, 51, 52
Trade Directories, 22–3, 38, 65
Transport, 5
Victorian Leeds, 7, 40, 56, 132, 139, 140, 144
Voting records, 23–4, 45
Wartime, 9, 10, 11, 13, 15, 16, 17

Index

West Yorkshire Archive Service
  Leeds, 18, 24, 33, 34–5, 44, 48, 50, 55, 62–4, 70, 72–5, 76, 83, 86, 88–9, 92, 100, 108, 147–8
West Yorkshire Archive Service
  Wakefield, 25–6, 42–3, 45–6, 76, 144–5, 148
Workhouse, 70–2, 73–5
Yorkshire Archaeological Society, 18–20, 24, 144